中华人民共和国文化和旅游部

2018年文化和旅游发展统计公报

STATISTICAL COMMUNIQUÉ OF THE MINISTRY OF CULTURE AND TOURISM OF THE PEOPLE'S REPUBLIC OF CHINA ON CULTURAL AND TOURISM DEVELOPMENT IN 2018

中华人民共和国文化和旅游部　编

中国统计出版社
China Statistics Press

图书在版编目（CIP）数据

中华人民共和国文化和旅游部 2018 年文化和旅游发展统计公报：汉英对照 / 中华人民共和国文化和旅游部编
. -- 北京：中国统计出版社，2019.5
ISBN 978-7-5037-8813-0

Ⅰ. ①中… Ⅱ. ①中… Ⅲ. ①文化发展－统计分析－公报－中国－2018－汉、英②旅游业－统计分析－公报－中国－2018－汉、英 Ⅳ. ① G12 ② F592

中国版本图书馆 CIP 数据核字 (2019) 第 077312 号

中华人民共和国文化和旅游部 2018 年文化和旅游发展统计公报

作　　者 / 中华人民共和国文化和旅游部
责任编辑 / 李　冲
装帧设计 / 黄　晨
出版发行 / 中国统计出版社
通信地址 / 北京市西城区月坛南街 57 号
邮政编码 / 100826
办公地址 / 北京市丰台区西三环南路甲 6 号
网　　址 / http://www.zgtjcbs.com
电　　话 /（010）63376907（发行部）
印　　刷 / 北京画中画印刷有限公司
经　　销 / 新华书店
开　　本 / 880×1230 毫米　1/16
字　　数 / 50 千字
印　　张 / 3
版　　别 / 2019 年 5 月第 1 版
版　　次 / 2019 年 5 月北京第 1 次印刷
定　　价 / 28.00 元

目录

CONTENTS

中华人民共和国文化和旅游部 2018 年文化和旅游发展统计公报[1]

2018 年，是决胜全面建成小康社会、实施“十三五”规划承上启下的关键一年。全国文化和旅游系统坚持以习近平新时代中国特色社会主义思想为指导，全面贯彻落实党的十九大和十九届二中、三中全会精神，紧紧围绕统筹推进“五位一体”总体布局和协调推进“四个全面”战略布局，增强“四个意识”，坚定“四个自信”，做到“两个维护”，坚持稳中求进的工作总基调，坚持以人民为中心的工作导向，大力推动文化事业、文化产业和旅游业融合发展，艺术创作持续繁荣，公共服务体系不断健全，市场管理规范有序，产业发展势头良好，社会主义核心价值观和中华优秀传统文化广泛弘扬，国家文化软实力和中华文化影响力大幅提升。

一、机构和人员

图 1　2014 年 –2018 年全国文化和旅游单位及人员情况

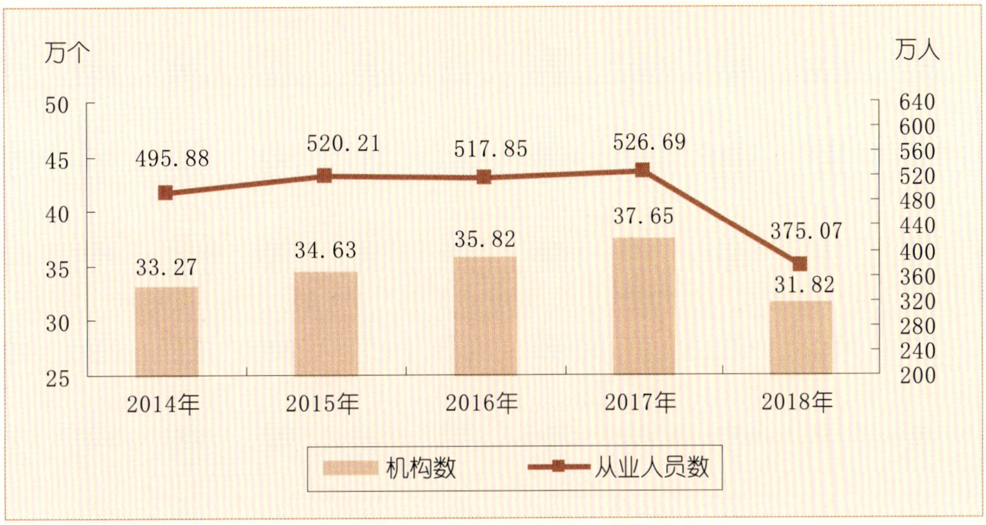

注：2018 年机构和从业人员暂未包括星级饭店和旅行社数据。

2018年末，纳入统计范围的全国各类文化和旅游单位[2]31.82万个，从业人员[3]375.07万人。其中，各级文化和旅游部门所属单位66835个，增加91个；从业人员67.06万人，增加0.34万人。

二、艺术创作演出

2018年，全国艺术院团继续开展“深入生活、扎根人民”工作，坚持以人民为中心的创作导向，树立精品意识，攀登艺术高峰。根据对全国400家重点统计艺术院团统计，2018年共创排艺术作品1150部，其中新创802部，复排260部，移植改编88部。国家直属院团精心创作，推出京剧《红军故事》、话剧《船歌》、童话芭蕾舞剧《九色鹿》、交响音乐会《浦东交响》等优秀作品，其中新创民族歌剧《刘三姐》以舞台艺术的形式展现桂林的“绿水青山”，成为推动文化和旅游融合的一次有益尝试。开展国家舞台艺术精品创作扶持工程，组织专家对入选的25部名录剧目进行打磨提升。实施西部及少数民族地区艺术创作提升计划和中国民族歌剧传承发展工程，扎实推进戏曲振兴、中国京剧像音像和剧本扶持工程以及戏曲剧本孵化计划，启动“时代交响－中国交响音乐作品创作扶持计划”，开展“主题歌曲＋”创作采风活动，组织创作了《抒情新时代－庆祝改革开放40周年新创歌曲音乐会》。成功组织庆祝改革开放40周年文艺晚会《我们的四十年》，精心组织开展2018年全国舞台艺术优秀剧目展演和全国优秀民族歌剧展演、全国优秀现实题材舞台艺术作品展（巡）演、全国基层院团戏曲会演、国家艺术院团演出季、全国美术馆馆藏精品展出季等系列艺术活动，集中展示优秀艺术成果。在元旦和春节期间，开展“文化科技卫生三下乡”“我们的中国梦－文化进万家”“文化迎春、艺术为民－文化和旅游部艺术家慰问基层”等系列活动。国家艺术基金立项一般资助项目

表1　2010年－2018年全国艺术表演团体基本情况

年　份	机构数（个）	从业人员数（人）	演出场次（万场）	国内演出观众人次（万人次）	总收入（万元）	
						#演出收入
2010年	6864	185413	137.15	88455.80	1239255	342696
2011年	7055	226599	154.72	74585.05	1540263	526745
2012年	7321	242047	135.02	82805.09	1968802	641480
2013年	8180	260865	165.11	90064.26	2800266	820738
2014年	8769	262887	173.91	91019.68	2264046	757028
2015年	10787	301840	210.78	95798.99	2576483	939313
2016年	12301	332920	230.60	118137.67	3112276	1308591
2017年	15742	402969	293.57	124739.06	3419618	1476786
2018年	17123	416374	312.46	137568.42	3667258	1522685

944 项，滚动资助项目 16 项，资助总额约为 7.6 亿元，有效发挥了推动优秀作品创作和优秀人才成长的孵化器作用。

年末全国共有艺术表演团体[4]17123 个，比上年末增加 1381 个，从业人员 41.64 万人，增加 1.34 万人。其中各级文化和旅游部门所属的艺术表演团体 2078 个，占 12.1%，从业人员 11.44 万人，占 27.5%。

全年全国艺术表演团体共演出 312.46 万场，比上年增长 6.4%，其中赴农村演出 178.82 万场，赴农村演出场次占总演出场次的 57.2%；国内观众 13.76 亿人次，比上年增长 10.3%，其中农村观众 7.79 亿人次；总收入 366.73 亿元，比上年增长 7.2%，其中演出收入 152.27 亿元，增长 3.1%。

全年全国文化和旅游部门所属艺术表演团体共组织政府采购公益演出 16.16 万场，观众 1.28 亿人次，分别比上年增长 2.7% 和 0.3%。利用流动舞台车演出 11.80 万场次，观众 0.95 亿人次，分别比上年增长 1.6% 和 0.2%。

年末全国共有艺术表演场馆 2478 个，比上年末增加 23 个。观众坐席数 192.04 万个，比上年增长 6.9%。全年共举行艺术演出 17.89 万场次，降低 15.5%；艺术演出观众人次 5862 万人次，降低 8.2%；艺术演出收入 37.44 亿元，降低 13.5%。其中各级文化和旅游部门所属艺术表演场馆 1236 个，比上年减少 17 个。全年共举行艺术演出 6.02 万场次，降低 15.2%；艺术演出观众人次 2588 万人次，降低 4.6%。

年末全国美术馆 528 个，比上年末增加 29 个，从业人员 4744 人，增加 168 人。全年共举办展览 7021 次，比上年增长 3.9%，参观人次 3721 万人次，与去年基本持平。

三、公共服务体系

2018 年，进一步贯彻落实《中华人民共和国公共文化服务保障法》《中华人民共和国公共图书馆法》，开展公共文化服务保障法贯彻落实情况督察，切实推动法律和各项改革举措落地生根。国家古籍保护工程深入推进，全球汉籍合璧工程、《中华医藏》《中华续道藏》确认立项并启动实施。推动各地在有条件的地区因地制宜开展县级文化馆、图书馆总分馆制建设和公共图书馆、文化馆法人治理结构改革试点。开展乡镇综合文化站专项治理，完成第三批国家公共文化服务体系示范区（项目）验收、第四批示范区（项目）创建和第六次全国县级以上公共图书馆评估定级工作，持续提升公共文化服务效能。推进国家公共文化云建设，完善共享直播、资源点播、大数据分析等功能。持续开展全国基层文化队伍培训，培训超 50 万人次。大力开展戏曲进乡村工作，为国家级贫困地区 12984 个乡镇配送了 77094 场文艺演出。组织全国广场舞展演活动，共举办展演活动 6225 场，参演团队 64564 支，参演群众达 209.4 万人，吸引超过 4206 万人次观看。举办第七届中国农民歌会、第九届中国少年儿童合唱节，开展“歌声伴着我成长”第五批全国新创少儿歌曲征集推广活动。持续开展面向革命老区、边疆地区、民族地区、贫困地区的“春雨工程”“阳光工程”“圆梦工程”文化志愿服务活动。举办“文化暖心”慰问演出活动，引导带动各地加大对特殊群体文化权益的保障力度。务实推进厕所革命工作，在厕所革命建设、技术应用、管理体制创新和文明提升行动方面稳步推进。

（一）公共图书馆[5]

年末全国共有公共图书馆3176个，比上年末增加10个。年末全国公共图书馆从业人员57602人，比上年末增加35人。其中具有高级职称的人员6632人，占11.5%；具有中级职称的人员18622人，占32.3%。

年末全国公共图书馆实际使用房屋建筑面积1595.98万平方米，比上年末增长5.3%；图书总藏量[6]103716万册，增长7.0%；阅览室坐席数111.68万个，增长4.9%；计算机22.35万台，其中供读者使用的电子阅览终端14.63万台，均与上年基本持平。

年末全国平均每万人公共图书馆建筑面积114.4平方米，比上年末增加5.4平方米；全国人均图书藏量0.74册，增加0.04册；全年全国人均购书费1.77元，增加0.07元。

图2　2010年–2018年全国公共图书馆人均资源情况

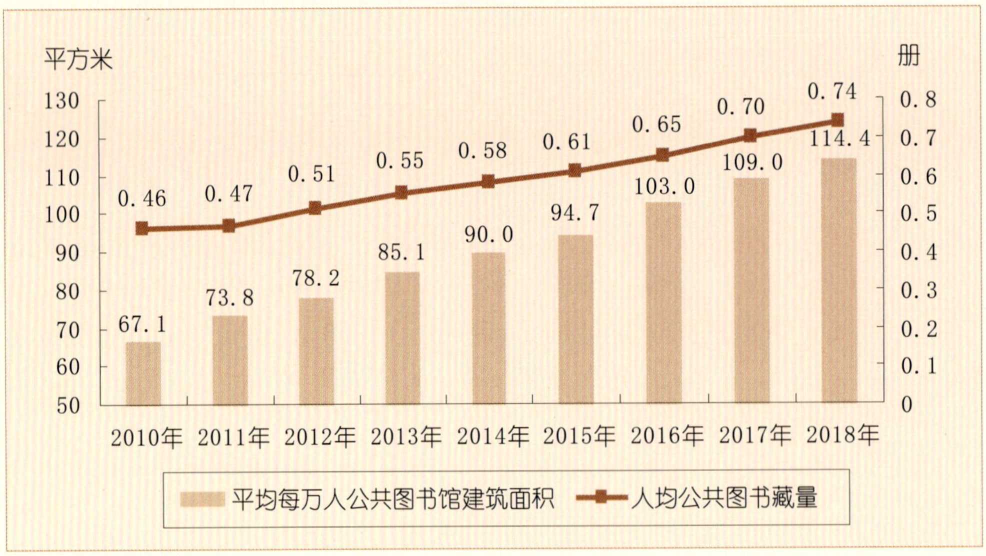

全年全国公共图书馆发放借书证[7]7263万个，比上年增长7.8%；总流通人次[8]82032万，增长10.2%。书刊文献外借册次58010万，增长5.3%；外借人次25814万，增长1.2%。全年共为读者举办各种活动179043次，增长15.1%；参加人次10648万，增长20.2%。

图 3　2010 年 –2018 年全国公共图书馆总流通人次及书刊外借册次

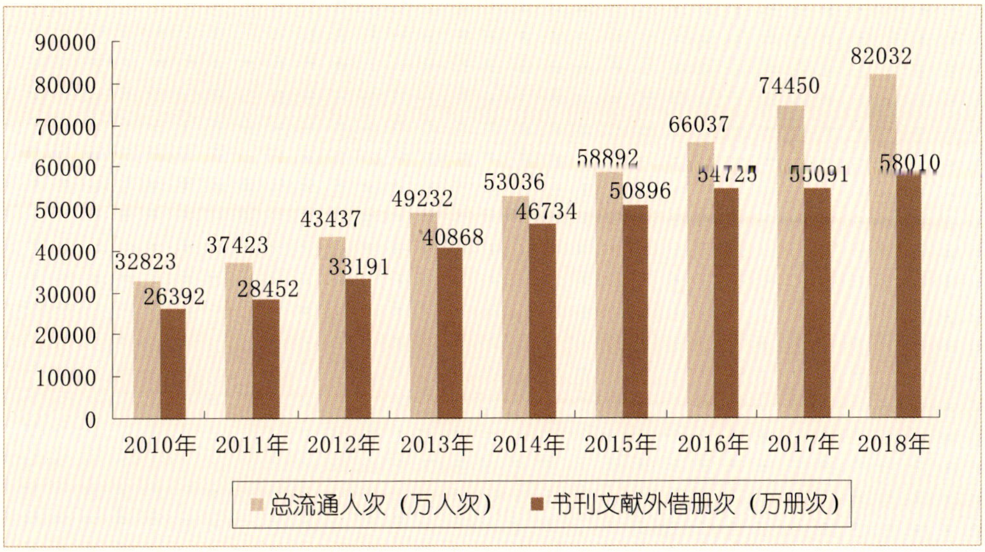

（二）**群众文化机构** [9]

年末全国共有群众文化机构 44464 个，比上年末减少 57 个。其中乡镇综合文化站 33858 个，比上年末减少 139 个。年末全国群众文化机构从业人员 185637 人，比上年末增加 4726 人。其中具有高级职称的人员 6386 人，占 3.4%；具有中级职称的人员 17245 人，占 9.3%。

年末全国群众文化机构实际使用房屋建筑面积 4283.07 万平方米，比上年末增长 4.3%；业务用房面积 3146.17 万平方米，增长 5.7%。年末全国平均每万人群众文化设施建筑面积 306.95 平方米，比上年末提高 11.51 平方米。

图 4　2010 年 –2018 年全国平均每万人群众文化设施建筑面积

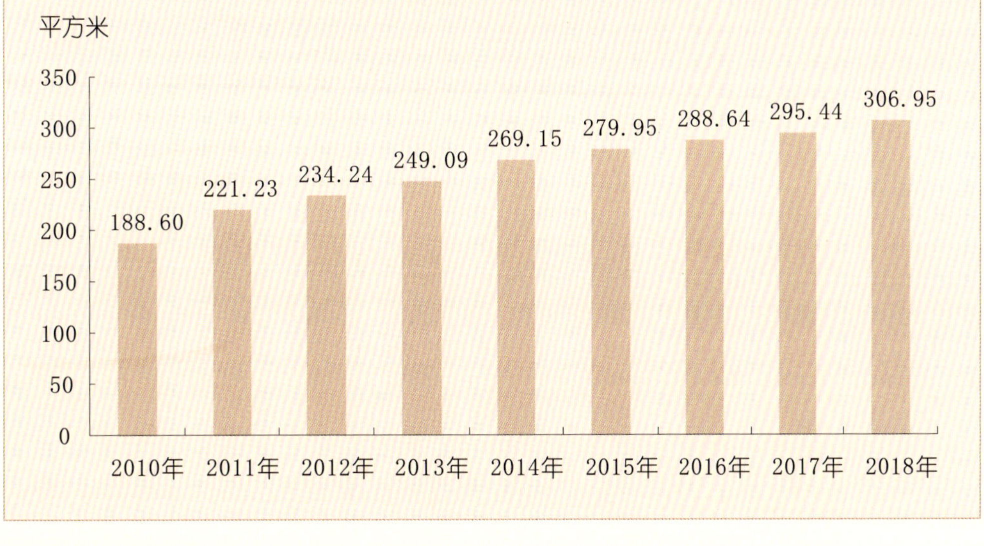

全年全国群众文化机构共组织开展各类文化活动[10]219.48 万场次，比上年增长 10.9%；服务人次 70553 万，增长 10.3%。

表 2　2018 年全国群众文化机构开展活动情况

项　目	总量		比上年增长（%）	
	活动次数（万次）	服务人次（万人次）	活动次数	服务人次
各项活动总计	219.48	70553	10.9	10.3
其中：展览	15.87	11037	3.0	3.0
文艺活动	123.12	53938	10.5	11.9
公益性讲座	3.58	618	4.1	9.8
训练班	76.90	4961	13.8	10.4

年末全国群众文化机构共有馆办文艺团体[11]7990 个，演出 16.30 万场，观众 8312 万人次。由文化馆（站）指导的群众业余文艺团体 42.61 万个，馆办老年大学 798 个。

四、文化和旅游市场管理

2018 年，进一步实施源头治理，支持引导文化市场经营单位改进服务、转变形象，修订《全国文化市场黑名单管理办法》《旅游市场黑名单管理办法（试行）》，研究制定《关于实施旅游服务质量提升计划的指导意见》《在线旅游经营服务管理暂行规定》，为提升质量、规范管理提供政策保障。旅行社、游艺娱乐场所等 9 项行政审批事项列入国务院“证照分离”改革事项并向全国推开。出台《文化和旅游部关于实施自由贸易试验区文化市场管理政策的通知》，支持自由贸易试验区和海南等地扩大文化和旅游市场开放。全面启用全国旅游监管服务平台，智能化监管水平进一步提升。推动出台《互联网上网服务营业场所服务等级评定》，开展“健康娱乐全民赛”“卡拉 OK 夕阳红”等活动，不断深化文化娱乐和上网服务行业转型升级，推进行业高质量发展。旅游安全和假日工作稳步推进，围绕“五一”“十一”和暑期、汛期等重点时段，加大对旅行社、A 级旅游景区安全检查和安全隐患排查力度。

年末全国文化市场经营单位[12]23.71 万家，比上年末减少 2.03 万家；从业人员 166.73 万人，减少 6.59 万人。其中全国共有娱乐场所 70584 个，从业人员 52.82 万人，全年营业收入 520.97 亿元，营业利润 112.33 亿元；互联网上网服务营业场所 124266 个，从业人员 34.67 万人，全年营业收入 294.63 亿元，营业利润 76.76 亿元。

综合执法业务能力不断提升，举办第二届全国文化市场综合执法岗位练兵技能竞赛，加大各类线上线下培训力度，举办各类培训 13 期，在线培训人员近 3 万人次，举办线上考试 600 余场。全国文化市场技术监管与服务平台投入运行，全国 97% 以上的省市县执法机构正式应用，2018 年通过平台出动检查 570.83 万人次，办结案件 3.64 万件。进一步扩大移动执法系统应用范围，全国已有 143 个地市上线应用，通过移动执法系统检查 4.2 万人次，检查经营单位 6880 次。加大市场执法检查和整治力度，持续开展各类专项整治行动，对营业性演出、网络表演、网络音乐、网络动漫等领域进行重点整治。加大旅游市场重点案件督办力度，督促处理涉旅投诉案件 2000 多起。全国共检查旅行社及其分支机构 6.76 万次，立案 3282 件，罚款及没收违法所得 3481 万元，吊销旅行社业务经营许可证 108 家。积极引导和推动“1+3”旅游市场综合监管机制建设，目前各地已设立旅游警察机构 437 家，工商旅游分局 344 家，旅游巡回法庭 554 家。

五、旅游资源利用

按照党中央、国务院关于全域旅游工作的安排部署，切实抓好《国务院办公厅关于促进全域旅游发展的指导意见》贯彻落实，依据《全域旅游示范区创建工作导则》，扎实推进国家全域旅游示范区创建工作，启动制定《国家全域旅游示范区验收、认定和管理实施办法（试行）》《国家全域旅游示范区验收标准（试行）》等文件，不断推进全域旅游向纵深发展，加快旅游业转型升级，提质增效。

印发《关于促进乡村旅游可持续发展的指导意见》《促进乡村旅游发展提质升级行动方案（2018 年—2020 年）》，推进乡村旅游持续健康发展。加强贫困地区旅游人才培训，全年共举办 9 期旅游扶贫培训班，培训 2000 人次，努力提高乡村旅游重点村干部、旅游带头人的知识水平和专业技能。

大力推进休闲度假旅游发展，为适应我国居民休闲度假旅游需求快速发展需要，积极营造有效的休闲度假空间，组织开展了国家级旅游度假区评定工作。持续推进中医药健康旅游发展，联合国家中医药管理局公布了第一批 72 家国家中医药健康旅游示范基地创建单位。大力发展自驾车旅居车旅游，加快推进自驾车游相关行业标准编制工作。加快发展温泉旅游、冰雪旅游等旅游新业态。

大力推进红色旅游工作，召开全国红色旅游五好讲解员建设行动推进会，在部分省份开展试点工作。与中宣部联合举办全国红色故事讲解员大赛，开展“金牌讲解员讲红色故事”集中展示活动，制作百部红色经典故事短视频进行集中展播。开展 6 期红色旅游示范性培训，培训红色旅游行政人员、景区和旅行社负责人、骨干讲解员、导游员 1300 余人。

统筹指导国内旅游市场开发与宣传推广工作，2018 年 11 月启动“全国冬季旅游推广季”活动，印发《关于做好冬季旅游产品供给工作的通知》。组织召开冬季旅游推广工作座谈会，举办“冬季旅游推广季启动仪式暨北国冰雪主题推介会”。围绕长江国际黄金旅游带发展推介会、全国新晋 5A 级旅游景区授牌仪式、中国旅游产业博览会等活动，组织新闻媒体进行集中报道，扩大活动社会影响力。

2018 年国内旅游市场持续平稳增长，入境旅游市场稳步进入缓慢回升通道，出境旅游市场快速发展。全年国内旅游人数 55.39 亿人次，比上年同期增长 10.8%；入境旅游人数 14120 万人次，比上年同期增长 1.2%；出境旅游人数 14972 万人次，比上年同期增长 14.7%；全年实现旅游总收入 5.97 万亿元，同比增长 10.5%。

表 3　2010 年 –2018 年旅游业主要发展指标

年　份	国内旅游人次（亿人次）	国内旅游收入（亿元）	入境旅游人次（万人次）	入境旅游收入（亿美元）	出境旅游人次（万人次）	旅游总收入（万亿元）
2010 年	21.03	12580	13376	458.14	5739	1.57
2011 年	26.41	19305	13542	484.64	7025	2.25
2012 年	29.57	22706	13241	500.28	8318	2.59
2013 年	32.62	26276	12908	516.64	9819	2.95
2014 年	36.11	30312	12850	1053.80	10728	3.73
2015 年	39.90	34195	13382	1136.50	11689	4.13
2016 年	44.35	39390	13844	1200.00	12203	4.69
2017 年	50.01	45661	13948	1234.17	13051	5.40
2018 年	55.39	51278	14120	1271.03	14972	5.97

年末全国共有 A 级景区 11924 个，全年接待总人数 60.24 亿人次，增长 10.5%，实现旅游收入 4707.54 亿元，增长 7.8%。

六、产业与科技

2018 年，印发《关于文化领域推广政府和社会资本合作模式的指导意见》，进一步推动政府职能转变，创新文化供给机制，引导社会资本积极投资文化领域。起草《关于完善促进消费体制机制进一步激发居民消费潜力的若干意见》和《完善促进消费体制机制实施方案（2018—2020 年）》，实施国家文化消费试点城市奖励计划，统筹推进文化和旅游消费工作。

组织中国文化艺术政府奖第三届动漫奖评奖，评选出 20 个奖项，引领动漫创作导向，激励原创动漫发展。组织制订“数字化艺术品图像显示系统的应用场景、框架和元数据”、“文物／艺术品 AR 需求及应用框架”等两项数字艺术标准，成功在国际电信联盟立项，为我国数字艺术产业走出去开辟道路。年末经文化和旅游部、财政部、国家税务总局三部门联合认定的动漫企业共有 809 个，重点动漫企业 43 个。

引导社会资本积极投资文化和旅游领域，联合财政部先后印发在文化、旅游领域推广政府和社会资本合作的政策文件，会同财政部评选的文化和旅游PPP（政府和社会资本合作）示范项目累计达到66个，获得“以奖代补”支持3.64亿元。

实施“文化产业双创扶持计划”，遴选扶持40家文化产业众创空间、双创服务平台，为民营文化企业、中小文化企业发展构建双创服务体系。印发《国家级文化产业示范园区创建验收标准(试行)》，明确创建验收工作的指标及具体内容，进一步加强创建工作的规范性。组织实施“国家级文化产业园区服务能力提升计划”，支持15个国家级文化产业园区的服务能力提升项目。

深化文化产业国际合作，推动更高水平对外开放。开展2018年“一带一路”文化贸易与投资重点项目征集与扶持工作，首批支持40个重点项目，涉及投资总额约42亿元，已陆续在沿线近10国落地实施。举办中加、中越、中日韩文化产业论坛和政策对话。支持文化企业“抱团出海”，全年共组织200余家文化企业以“中国展区”形式参加美国国际授权博览会等9个重点国际文化展会。协调组织首届中国国际进口博览会文化和旅游领域招商招展、旅行保障等系列工作，支持举办“合生共振”文化＋科技高峰论坛配套活动，搭建企业对外交流合作新平台。加强文化产业国际人才培养与交往，通过举办中国文化产品国际营销年会系列论坛，培训涉外文化经营管理人员近2000人次。

根据国家统计局统计，2018年全国6.0万家规模以上文化及相关产业企业实现营业收入89257亿元，比上年增长8.2%，持续保持较快增长。

2018年，组织实施文化创新工程，继续开展文化和旅游部重点实验室资助项目评审工作。开展2018年度全国艺术科学规划项目评审立项工作，坚持以文化和旅游建设重大理论和现实问题为主攻方向，进一步发挥项目示范引导作用。着力推动文化和旅游智库体系建设，以《文化和旅游智库要报》为主渠道，加强研究成果转化应用，发挥研究成果的决策咨询作用。成功举办第三届全国“梨花杯”青少年戏曲教育教学成果展示活动，高质量高规格地集中展示近年来我国戏曲教育水平和最新教学成果。

七、文化遗产保护利用

2018年，国家文物局认真贯彻习近平总书记关于文物工作的重要指示精神，深入落实《关于进一步加强文物工作的指导意见》《关于加强文物保护利用改革的若干意见》，扎实推进文物保护各项重点工作。完成《长城保护总体规划》《长征文化线路保护总体规划》和《大运河文化带建设总体规划纲要》。启动第八批全国重点文物保护单位申报遴选，开展全国重点文物保护本体构成核定、省级文物保护单位名录整理工作。开展县级国家历史文化名城文物保护评估，推进馆藏文物预防性保护和数字化保护。经远舰、“上海长江口二号”沉船遗址水下考古项目取得重要进展，西藏旧石器遗址、陕西石峁、芦山峁遗址、新疆石城子遗址获重大发现。开展互联网＋中华文明行动计划，推动与腾讯、百度、网易、中国移动等战略合作深度拓展。对全国博物馆和文物建筑消防安全进行督促检查，共检查博物馆和文物建筑 3.1 万家，整改火灾隐患 6.1 万余处。持续推进文物法人违法案件专项整治行动，查处 673 起文物法人违法案件，行政处罚 349 起，责令改正 408 起，行政追责 314 人次，刑事追责 74 人次，督办一批涉及革命文物、世界文化遗产等违法案件。截至 2018 年末，全国共有可移动文物 1.08 亿件／套，不可移动文物 76.7 万处。

年末全国共有各类文物机构 10160 个，比上年末增加 229 个。其中，文物保护管理机构 3550 个，占 34.9%，博物馆[13]4918 个，占 48.4%。年末全国文物机构从业人员 16.26 万人，比上年末增加 0.11 万人。其中高级职称 9682 人，占 6.0%，中级职称 20679 人，占 12.7%。

图 5　2010 年 –2018 年全国文物机构及从业人员情况

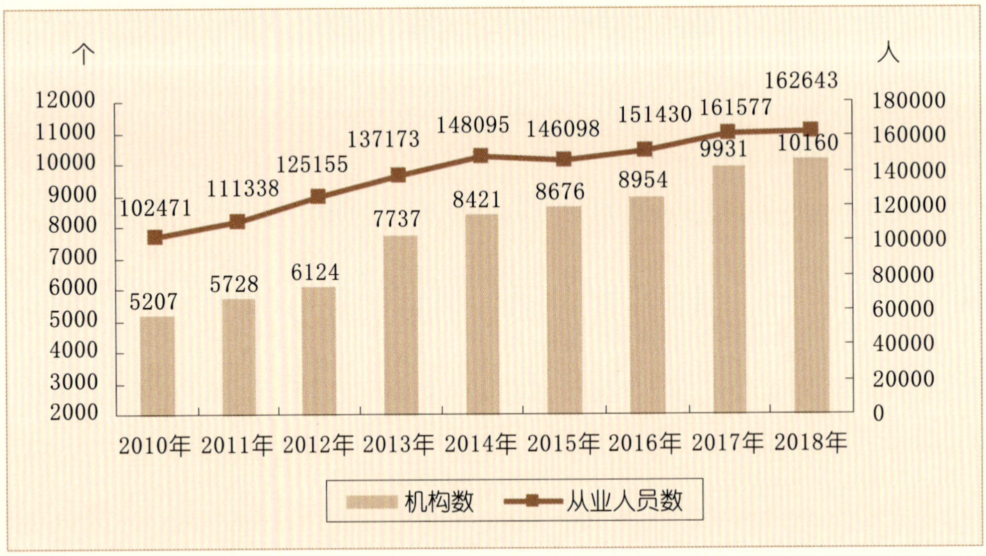

年末全国文物机构拥有文物藏品 4960.61 万件，比上年末增加 109.95 万件／套，增长 2.3%。其中，博物馆文物藏品 3754.25 万件／套，占文物藏品总量的 75.7%；文物商店文物藏品 751.40 万件／套，占 15.2%。

2018 年全国各类文物机构共举办陈列展览 27919 个，比上年增加 1874 个。其中，基本陈列[14]13676 个，比上年增加 651 个；临时展览[15]14243 个，比上年增加 1223 个。接待观众 122387 万人次，比上年增长 6.6%，其中未成年人 29665 万人次，增长 2.6%，占参观总人数的 24.2%。博物馆接待观众 104436 万人次，增长 7.5%，占文物机构接待观众总数的 85.3%。

2018 年，加大非遗代表性项目和代表性传承人保护力度。“藏医药浴法”成功列入联合国教科文组织人类非物质文化遗产代表作名录。截至 2018 年末，我国共有 40 个项目列入联合国教科文组织人类非物质文化遗产名录（册）。对涉及中华文明发源地、文化发祥地的国家级非遗代表性项目开展研究，全面记录 103 名国家级非遗代表性传承人，评估验收 2016 年支持的 253 个记录项目。

图 6 2010 年 –2018 年全国文物机构接待观众人次及未成年人观众人次

贯彻落实传统工艺振兴计划，推动传统工艺在现代生活中得到新的广泛应用。制定第一批国家传统工艺振兴目录，共有 14 个门类的 383 个项目入选。指导各地制定本地区传统工艺振兴计划，共有 24 个省（区、市）出台本地区传统工艺振兴计划或相关文件。支持传统工艺工作站驻站单位举办 12 场传承人对话活动，促成传承人与设计企业、高校等机构的多项跨界合作。

完善研培工作机制，拓展覆盖范围，深入实施中国非遗传承人群研修研习培训计划。印发《中国非物质文化遗产传承人群研修研习培训计划实施方案（2018–2020）》，确定 112 所院校参与 2018 年研培计划，全国累计举办各类研修、研习、培训班 628 期，培训学员 2.65 万人次，加上各地延伸培训，共计培训 9.5 万人次。继续探索新门类非遗项目的研培试点，支持中央民族大学在湖北举办民间文学类非遗传承人群研修交流活动。

认定并公布 1082 名第五批国家级非遗代表性传承人。截至 2018 年末，共有国家级非遗代表性传承人 3068 人，国家级非遗代表性项目 1372 项。进一步加强国家级非物质文化遗产保护利用设施建设，安排中央预算内投资 2.01 亿元支持建设 26 个国家级非遗保护利用设施，有效推动了非物质文化遗产保护传承与经济社会发展的有机结合。

创新传播方式，提升非遗传播专业水平，推动形成全社会传承发展优秀传统文化的良好局面。组织开展 2018 年“文化和自然遗产日”活动，全国共举办大中型非遗宣传展示活动 3700 多项。举办全国曲艺周，第一次在全国范围内将 127 个曲艺类国家级非遗代表性项目进行集中展演。制作播出《非遗公开课》，宣传非遗保护理念，普及非遗知识，社会反响热烈。开展非遗影像展、非遗服饰秀、非遗讲座月等品牌传播活动，线上线下共 2.6 亿人次参与。以“活态传承、活力再现”为主题，举办第五届中国非遗博览会，展示近年来全国非遗保护工作取得的进展，82 万人次到场参观，近 6000 万人次通过网络观看。支持和指导各地做好非遗活动进校园、非遗项目进课堂、非遗知识进教材，发挥非遗在青少年健康成长中的积极作用。

截至 2018 年末，全国共有非物质文化遗产保护机构 2467 个，从业人员 17308 人。全年全国各类非物质文化遗产保护机构举办演出 65495 场，增长 20.6%，观众 4960 万人次，增长 16.6%；举办民俗活动 16844 次，增长 24.0%，观众 4850 万人次，增长 0.7%。

八、文化和旅游对外及对港澳台交流

2018年，以文化和旅游双多边交流机制及高级别人文交流机制为抓手，与冈比亚、巴拿马、西班牙、尼日利亚等 18 国签署文化协定或执行计划，推动深化与世界各国的文化和旅游交流与合作。举办上海合作组织、中日韩、中美、中国—东盟等有关活动，参加中加、中意、中俄蒙和亚欧、亚太以及金砖国家等相关会议。

建立“一带一路”文化和旅游交流机制，成立丝绸之路国际博物馆联盟、国际图书馆联盟、美术馆联盟。举办第五届丝绸之路国际艺术节、第三届丝绸之路（敦煌）国际文化博览会、丝绸之路国家美术馆作品展。在“一带一路”沿线国家和地区打造“丝绸之路文化之旅”和“丝绸之路文化使者”等重点交流品牌，助力“一带一路”沿线国家民心相通。

以讲好中国故事为主线，提升“欢乐春节”文化交流品牌形象，2018 年“欢乐春节”在全球 130 个国家和地区的 400 多座城市举办近 2000 场活动。加强“超乎想象的中国”旅游推广，打造“美丽中国”旅游品牌。在阿维尼翁戏剧节、爱丁堡艺穗节等节展框架下举办“聚焦中国”系列活动。在美国、加拿大、俄罗斯、尼泊尔等国举办文化年（节）活动，进一步塑造“中国年节”形象品牌。

制定《文化和旅游部与地方合作共建海外中国文化中心工作指南》，加强驻外文化和旅游机构相关制度建设，在拉脱维亚、摩洛哥开设中国文化中心，使全球中国文化中心总数达到 37 个。与约旦、乌拉圭、阿联酋、科特迪瓦、阿尔及利亚、西班牙等 6 国签署设立文化中心的政府文件。继续开展部省共建中心工作，与广西壮族自治区、江西省签署合作共建河内中国文化中心、里斯本中国文化中心的协议。指导海外中国文化中心联动举办“中国文化周”统一品牌活动和“天涯共此时”中秋品牌活动。

积极开展对港澳台文化和旅游工作，推动粤港澳大湾区文化和旅游工作协调机制建设。举办第九届海峡两岸文化创意产业展、第 14 届海峡旅游博览会和第 11 届海峡两岸文博会。创新春节、中秋等节庆交流平台，提升“香江明月夜”“海峡两岸民俗庙会”等主题文化活动影响力。持续打造“艺海流金”、情系钱塘——两岸文化联谊行等文化交流品牌，组织“如意甘肃行”等旅游推广活动，举办台北夏季旅展等。持续开展港澳台青少年文化旅游实习研学等活动，培育港澳台青少年中华文化认同。

全年经文化系统审批的对外文化交流项目 3383 起，66734 人次参加；对港澳文化交流项目 490 项，11411 人次参加；对台文化交流项目 311 项，3642 人次参加。

九、资金投入

2018 年，中央财政通过继续实施“三馆一站”免费开放、非物质文化遗产保护、公共数字文化建设等文化项目，共落实中央补助地方文化专项资金 50.51 亿元，比上年增长 0.6%。

图 7　2010 年 –2018 年中央对地方文化项目补助资金情况

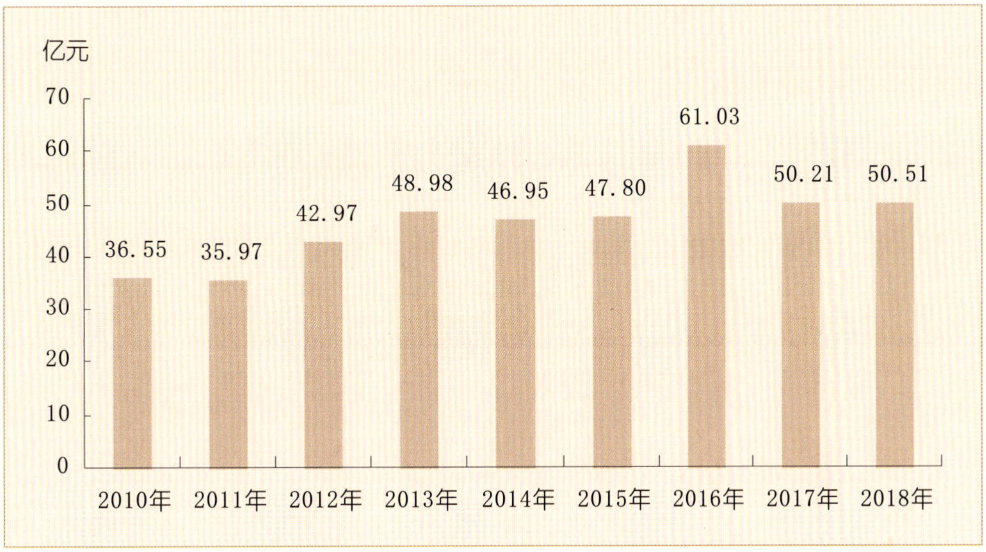

另外，中央财政安排旅游发展基金 14.85 亿元，对地方旅游厕所建设、全域旅游示范区创建及旅游公共服务体系和旅游业转型升级融合发展项目进行了重点支持。

全年全国文化事业费[16]928.33 亿元，比上年增加 72.53 亿元，增长 8.5%；全国人均文化事业费 66.53 元，比上年增加 4.96 元，增长 8.1%。

图 8　2010 年 –2018 年全国人均文化事业费及增速情况

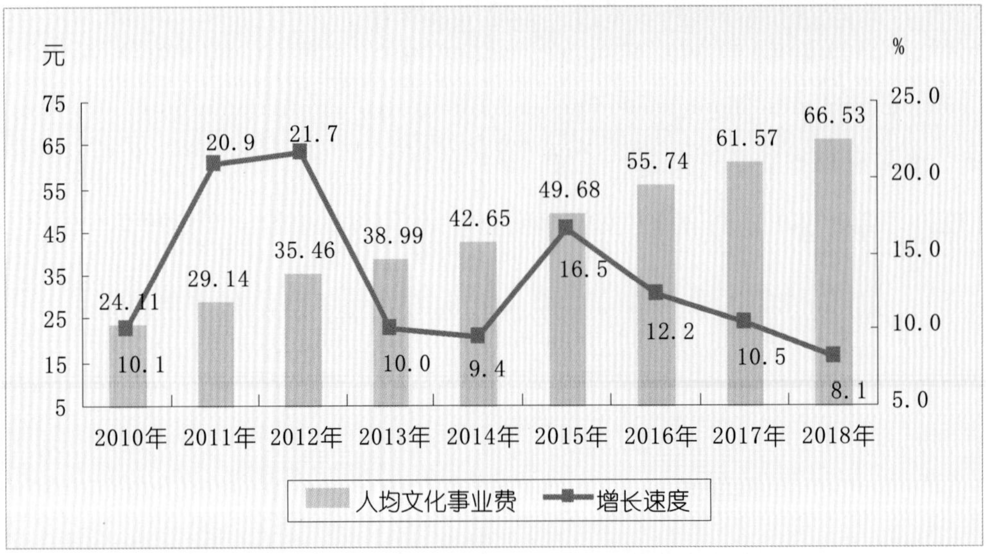

文化事业费占财政总支出的比重为 0.42%，比重和上年持平。

图 9　全国文化事业费占财政总支出比重

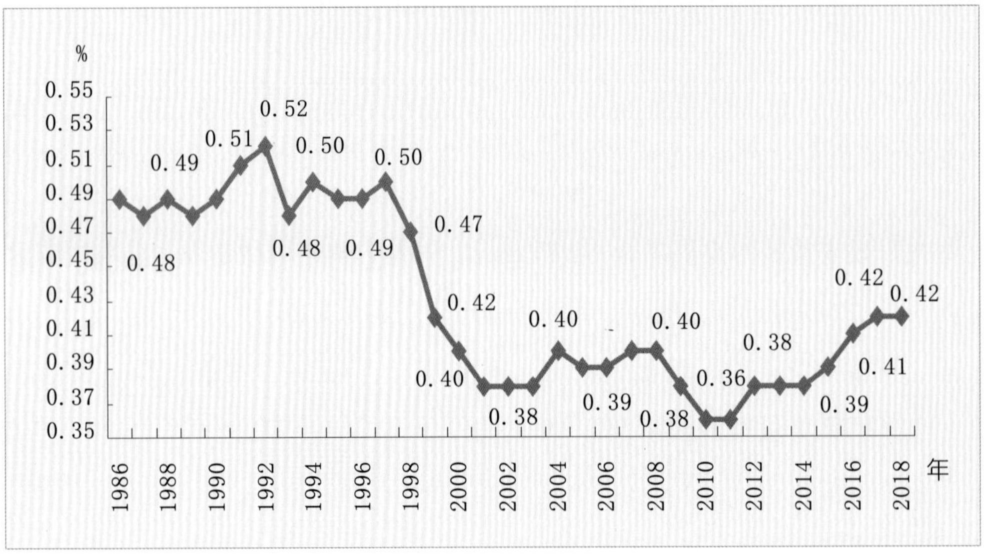

全国文化事业费中，县以上文化单位 424.96 亿元，占 45.8%，比重比上年降低了 0.7 个百分点；县及县以下文化单位 503.37 亿元，占 54.2%，比重比上年提高了 0.7 个百分点。东部地区[17]文化单位文化事业费 416.24 亿元，占 44.8%，比重提高了 0.2 个百分点；中部地区文化单位 232.71 亿元，占 25.1%，比重提高了 0.2 个百分点；西部地区文化单位 242.93 亿元，占 26.2%，比重下降了 0.8 个百分点。

全年全国文物事业费[18]378.79 亿元，比上年增加 29.57 亿元，增长 8.3%；文物事业费占财政总支出的比重为 0.17%，比重和上年持平。

表 4　全国文化事业费按城乡和区域分布情况

项　目		1995 年	2000 年	2005 年	2010 年	2015 年	2017 年	2018 年
总量（亿元）	全国	33.39	63.16	133.82	323.06	682.97	855.80	928.33
	#县以上	24.44	46.33	98.12	206.65	352.84	398.35	424.96
	县及县以下	8.95	16.87	35.70	116.41	330.13	457.45	503.37
	#东部地区	13.43	28.85	64.37	143.35	287.87	381.71	416.24
	中部地区	9.54	15.05	30.58	78.65	164.27	213.30	232.71
	西部地区	8.30	13.70	27.56	85.78	193.87	230.70	242.93
所占比重（%）	全国	100.0	100.0	100.0	100.0	100.0	100.0	100.0
	#县以上	73.2	73.4	73.3	64.0	51.7	46.5	45.8
	县及县以下	26.8	26.7	26.7	36.0	48.3	53.5	54.2
	#东部地区	40.2	45.7	48.1	44.4	42.1	44.6	44.8
	中部地区	28.6	23.8	22.9	24.3	24.1	24.9	25.1
	西部地区	24.9	21.7	20.6	26.6	28.4	27.0	26.2

据财政部统计，2018 年全国财政支出中，文化体育与传媒经费[19]3522 亿元，比上年增长 3.7%，占财政支出的 1.59%，比重比上年下降 0.07 个百分点。

图 10　2010 年 –2018 年全国文化体育与传媒经费总量及增长速度

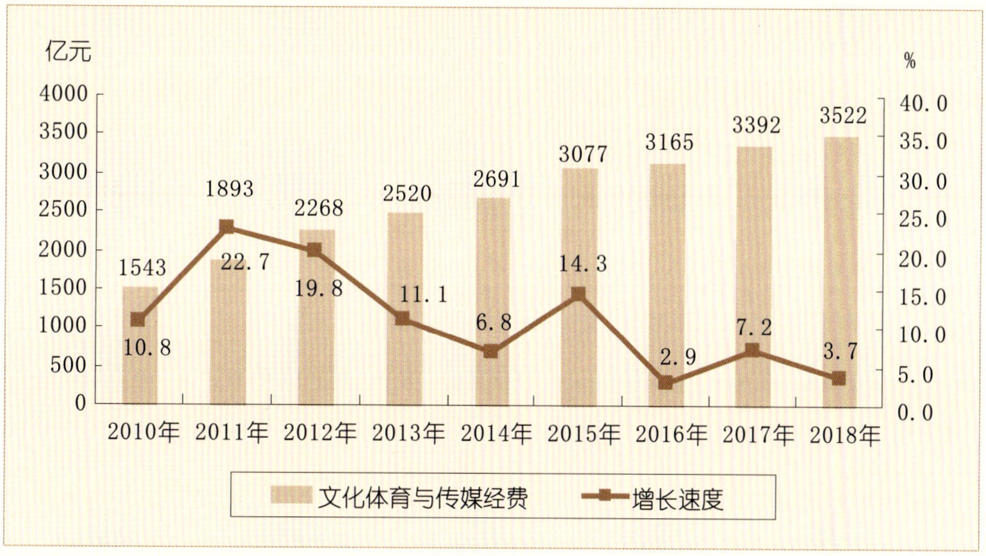

注释：

[1] 本公报中各项数据为初步统计数据。各项统计数据均未包括香港特别行政区、澳门特别行政区和台湾省。部分数据因四舍五入的原因，存在着与分项合计不等的情况。

[2] 文化和旅游单位是指全国各级文化和旅游部门主办的或实行行业管理的文化机构，不含各级新闻出版、广播影视等部门主办或管理的机构。根据现行的统计制度，各级文化和旅游部门主办单位（如公共图书馆、文化馆、文化站、博物馆、公有制艺术表演团体、公有制艺术表演场馆等）全部纳入了统计范围，实行行业管理的文化和旅游单位中，娱乐场所和互联网上网服务营业场所、非公有制艺术表演团体、非公有制艺术表演场馆、经营性互联网文化单位、艺术品经营机构和演出经纪机构和A级景区纳入了统计，星级饭店和旅行社数据暂未包括。

[3] 从业人员是指在各级文化和旅游部门主办或实行行业管理的机构中工作并取得劳动报酬的人员。

[4] 艺术表演团体指由文化和旅游部门主办或实行行业管理（经文化行政部门审批并领取营业性演出许可证），专门从事表演艺术等活动的各类专业艺术表演团体。

[5] 公共图书馆是指由各级文化和旅游部门主办的、面向社会公众开放并提供科学、文化等各种知识普及教育的机构。

[6] 公共图书馆总藏量指已编目的古籍、图书、期刊和报纸的合订本、手册、手稿，以及缩微制品、录像带、录音带、光盘等视听文献资料数量之和，不包括电子图书。

[7] 公共图书馆发放的借书证数是指由公共图书馆发放，并在当年内使用过至少一次的借书证数。

[8] 公共图书馆总流通人次是指本年度内到图书馆场馆接受图书馆服务的总人次，包括借阅书刊、咨询问题，以及参加各类读者活动等。

[9] 群众文化机构是指各级文化和旅游部门主办的开展群众文化活动的场所，主要包括文化馆（含综合性文化中心、群众艺术馆）、文化站。

[10] 群众文化机构组织开展活动是指组织文艺活动、举办训练班、举办展览和组织公益性讲座总和。

[11] 群众文化机构馆办文艺团体指由本馆人员组成的为群众提供文艺演出的演出团队。

[12] 文化市场经营单位指经文化市场行政部门审批或备案并领取相关许可或备案文件的、从事文化经营和文化服务活动的机构。按照现行统计制度，文化市场经营单位统计范围包括娱乐场所和互联网上网服务营业场所、非公有制艺术表演团体、非公有制艺术表演场馆、经营性互联网文化单位、艺术品经营机构和演出经纪机构。

[13] 博物馆指为了研究、教育、欣赏的目的，收藏、保护、展示人类活动和自然环境的见证物，

向公众开放，非营利性、永久性社会服务机构，包括以博物馆（院）、纪念馆（舍）、科技馆、陈列馆等专有名称开展活动的单位。

[14] 基本陈列指在本馆布置陈列、地点固定、时间较长的展出。

[15] 临时展览指在本机构内设置，由本馆设计布陈，形式比较多样的展出。

[16] 文化事业费是指区域内各级财政对文化和旅游系统主办单位的经费投入总和。根据现行统计口径，文化事业费不包括各级文化和旅游行政部门的行政运行经费。

[17] 东部地区包括北京、天津、辽宁、上海、江苏、浙江、福建、山东、广东；中部地区包括河北、山西、吉林、黑龙江、安徽、江西、河南、湖北、湖南、海南；西部地区包括内蒙古、广西、重庆、四川、贵州、云南、西藏、陕西、甘肃、青海、宁夏、新疆。

[18] 文物事业费是指区域内各级财政对文物事业的经费投入总和。一般包括博物馆、文物保护管理机构等文物事业单位的财政拨款（不含基建拨款）及文物部门所属企业的财政补贴。

[19] 文化体育与传媒经费数据源自财政部，是指各级政府在文化、文物、体育、广播影视和新闻出版方面的投入。

Statistical Communiqué of the Ministry of Culture and Tourism of the People's Republic of China on Cultural and Tourism Development in 2018[1]

The year 2018 was crucial to secure a decisive victory in building a moderately prosperous society in all respects and implement the country's 13th Five-Year Plan (2016-2020). In this year, under the guidance of the Thought on Socialism with Chinese characteristics for the new era put forward by President Xi Jinping, all governmental cultural and tourism departments in China have implemented and put into practice the guiding principles from the 19th CPC National Congress, the 2nd and 3rd Plenary Sessions of the 19th CPC Central Committee, and worked in accordance with the "Five-Pronged Overall Plan" and "Four Comprehensives" strategy to promote all-round economic, political, cultural, social, and ecological progress in China and with "Four Confidences" and "Two Commitments" in their mind. With the aim to strengthen the linkages between culture and tourism in a steady and progressive way, they put people at the center of their work with high sense of responsibility, disseminated socialist core values and the best of time-honored Chinese culture, augmented public cultural service system, encouraged vibrant cultural and creative productions and a regulated, orderly cultural market, and promoted the growth of cultural industries. Their work contributed a great deal in building a culturally strong China with remarkable visibility and cultural presence across the globe.

I. Institution and Employment

318,200 national cultural and tourism units[2] were brought into the statistical range by the end of 2018, and the number of employees[3] was 3.7507 million. Among them, 66,835 units were affiliated to government cultural and tourism departments, 91 more than those of the past year, with 670,600 employees, 3,400 persons more than those of the previous year.

Figure 1: Number of national cultural and tourism units and employed persons in 2014-2018

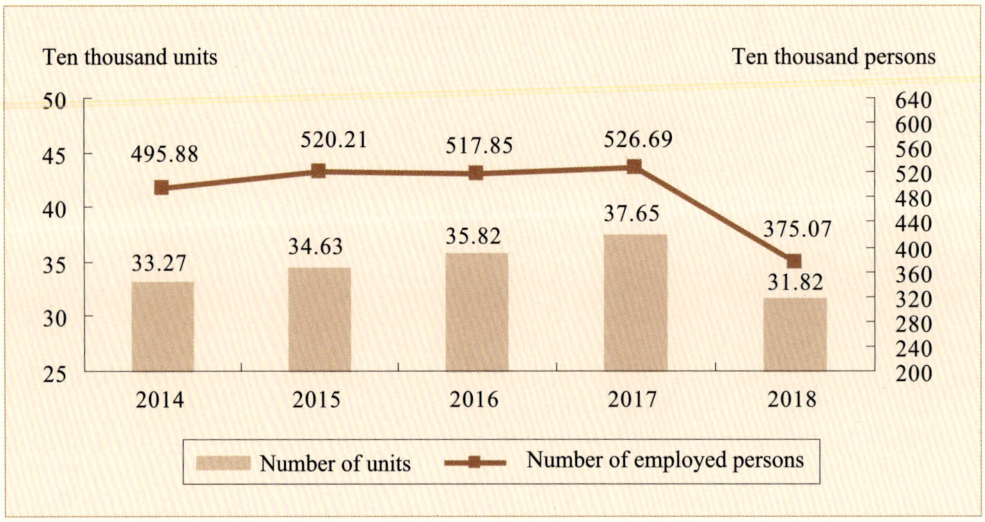

Note: The numbers of employees in star hotels and travel agencies are not included.

II. Performing Arts

In 2018, performing art troupes all across China continued to put the spirit of "drawing inspiration from real life and the people" into action, and put people at the center of their work, and endeavored to reach artistic excellence. According to the statistics of 400 major performing arts companies, in 2018, 1150 productions came out, among which 802 were new, 260 were remade, and 88 adapted or rearranged. The highlighted productions presented by national-level state-owned companies included Peking opera show *The Red Army,* drama *Song of Voyagers,* ballet *Nine-colored Deer,* and concert with Pudong, Shanghai as the theme. In particular, Chinese opera *Liu Sanjie* was a pioneer exploration to link performing arts, culture and tourism, as the landscape of Guilin was set to stage design and music. The projects to support excellent national performing arts productions, support artistic creativity in western regions and regions mainly inhabited by ethnic minorities, promote national operas, foster rejuvenation of traditional folk *xiqu* operas and creation of new scripts, encourage the development of Peking opera recordings and play scripts, and to support the production of symphony music were further carried out. In particular, we organized an expert panel to polish the 25 plays listed as productions of excellence. Following a program for writing new Reform-and-Opening-up-theme songs through study tours and workshops, we presented a concert of new songs written to celebrate the 40th anniversary of China's Reform and Opening up. For the same cause, we also successfully presented Our Forty Years, the commemoration cultural gala. Artistic excellence was presented in such programs as 2018 national show season for performing arts productions of excellence and national operas, tour of performing arts productions with realistic themes nationwide, collective shows of *xiqu* opera productions from grassroot theaters nationwide, national performing arts troupe show season, and 2018 exhibition season of national art museum collections. During the time of New Year and Chinese New Year, we have conducted programs to bring culture, technology and health services to rural areas, organize cultural activities in communities, and organize visits of artists to grassroot communities, supported by the Ministry of Culture and Tourism. Serving as a incubator of outstanding creativity and creative talents, National Arts Fund of China provided in total 760 million RMB as financial support to 944 new arts programs and 16 existing programs with new developments in 2018.

By the end of the year, the number of art performance troupes[4] reached 17,123, an increase of 1,381 over the end of the previous year; that of the professionals reached 416,400 with the increase of 13,400. Of them, the art performance troupes managed by cultural departments at all levels reached 2,078, accounting for 12.1% of the total with 114,400 art employees, which is 27.5% of the total.

In 2018, all art troupes in China presented 3.1246 million performances, an increase of 6.4% over the previous year; the domestic audiences reached 1.376 billion, up by 10.3%; the number of performances for audience in rural areas was 1.7882 million, accounting for 57.2% of the total; the number of the rural audiences was 779 million. The total turnover of the performing troupes was 36.673 billion yuan, an increase of 7.2% over the previous year; of them the income from performing arts was 15.227 billion yuan, up by 3.1%.

Table 1: General information of art troupes nationwide in 2010-2018

Year	Number of institutions (unit)	Number of employees (person)	Number of shows (ten thousand)	Number of domestic audience attendances (ten thousand)	Total income (ten thousand yuan)	
						#Shows' box office
2010	6864	185413	137.15	88455.80	1239255	342696
2011	7055	226599	154.72	74585.05	1540263	526745
2012	7321	242047	135.02	82805.09	1968802	641480
2013	8180	260865	165.11	90064.26	2800266	820738
2014	8769	262887	173.91	91019.68	2264046	757028
2015	10787	301840	210.78	95798.99	2576483	939313
2016	12301	332920	230.60	118137.67	3112276	1308591
2017	15742	402969	293.57	124739.06	3419618	1476786
2018	17123	416374	312.46	137568.42	3667258	1522685

The amount of government-purchased public performances presented by art performance troupes affiliated to official cultural and tourism departments throughout the year was 161,600, with audiences of 128 million, up by 2.7% and 0.3% respectively. The number of the performances on traveling stage vans was 118,000, with audience attendances of 95 million, up by 1.6% and 0.2% respectively.

By the end of the year, the venues of the performing arts amounted to 2,478, 23 more than those of the previous year, with 1,920,400 seats, increased by 6.9%. Among them, 1,236 are state-owned, down by 17 compared to that of previous year. 178,900 performances were held throughout the year, down by 15.5% over the previous year; the audiences reached 58.62 million, a decrease of 8.2%. 60,200 performances were held in the state-owned venues affiliated to the cultural and tourism departments throughout the year, down by 15.2% over the previous year; the audiences reached 25.88 million, a decrease of 4.6%. The total turnover of art performances reached 3.744 billion yuan, down by 13.5%.

By the end of 2018, there were 528 art museums affiliated to art administrations in China, 29 more than those of the previous year, with 4,744 employees, 168 than the previous year. 7,021 exhibitions were presented by these museums year-round, up by 3.9%, attracting 37.21 million visitor attendances, about the same with that of the previous year.

III. Public Cultural Service System

In 2018, further steps were taken to implement the laws on the public cultural service guarantee and on public libraries of the People' s Republic of China. We carried out inspections on the implementation of Law on Public Cultural Service Guarantee and key reform tasks mandated by the central government, and made sure that legislation and reform measures were translated into real results. Efforts were made to carry out the national project to preserve ancient books and manuscripts, and projects including global integration program of books written in Chinese, the documentation of Chinese medical books, and the second-phase documentation of Taoist books were confirmed and initiated. We encouraged provinces and cities with adequate conditions to set up main-branch system of cultural centers and libraries, and initiate legal person governance structure reform in public libraries and cultural centers. With the commitment to efficiency, we carried out governance improvement program for township-level cultural stations, completed the review and acceptance of the 3rd batch of national public cultural service system pilot zones and programs, the confirmation of the 4th batch, and the 6th nationwide evaluation of public libraries at or above township-level. Further steps were made in building cloud public cultural service system, enriching it with shared streaming, a-la-carte content, and big data analysis mechanism. We continued to promote public cultural service capacity building, and trained more than 500,000 people. In our efforts to put *xiqu* opera shows in rural villages, we organized 77.094 cultural and art shows in 12,984 towns and villages in the poverty-stricken areas. Public square dancing shows were organized across the country. 6,225 shows presented by 64,564 teams and 2.094 million dancers have attracted over 42.06 million audience attendances. We hosted the 7th Farmer's Singing Competition and 9th Choir Festival for Children and Young People, and carried out the 5th program to commission and promote newly written children's songs. Cultural volunteer projects including Spring Rain, Sunshine and Dream were continued to target regions of revolutionary heritage, border regions, regions mainly inhabited by ethnic minorities and poverty-stricken areas. We also presented free art galas as part of our efforts to encourage local governments to work harder to guarantee the cultural rights of under-privileged groups. Substantial work has been done to step up the "toilet revolution", including building stronger human resource capacity, introducing new technology and managerial structures, and raising public awareness of keeping toilets clean and tidy.

(1) Public Libraries[5]

By the end of the year, there were in total 3,176 libraries nationwide, 10 more than the number of the previous year. The total number of employees of public libraries across China reached 57,602, 35 more than the number of the previous year. Among them, 6,632 owned senior professional titles, accounting for 11.5%, and 18,622 owned medium-level professional titles, accounting for 32.3%.

According to statistics at the end of 2018, the actual floor space used by public library buildings totaled 15.9598 million m^2, up by 5.3% over the end of the previous year. 1.03716 billion books[6] were collected in these libraries, up by 7.0%. The number of seats in reading rooms was 1.1168 million, up by 4.9%, and that of computers was 223,500, and that of electronic reading terminals for readers was 146,300, about the same as those numbers of the previous year.

By the end of the 2018 the floor space of public libraries for each ten thousand persons was 114.4 m^2, an increase of 5.4 m^2 over the end of the previous year; the number of books per capita was 0.74, an increase of 0.04 over the previous year; the money spent on books per capita was 1.77 yuan, an increase of 0.07 yuan over previous year.

Figure 2: Information of per capita resource of national public libraries in 2010-2018

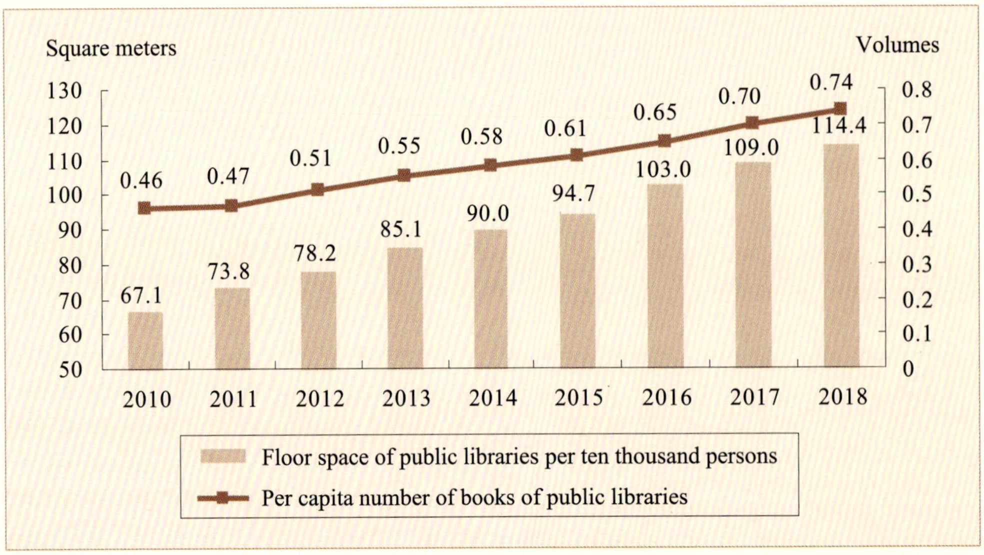

In 2018, library cards[7] issued by public libraries across the country throughout the year total to 72.63 million, increased by 7.8%; the total flow of person-time[8] reached 820.32 million, a growth of 10.2%. The total circulation number of books, magazines, and documents loaned to readers reached 580.1 million, up by 5.3%; a total of 258.11 million person times borrowed books, a growth of 1.2%. Various activities organized for readers total to 179,043, up by 15.1%; which attracted 106.48 million person-times, an increase of 20.2%.

Figure 3: Total flow of person-time and number of books lent out of national public libraries in 2010-2018

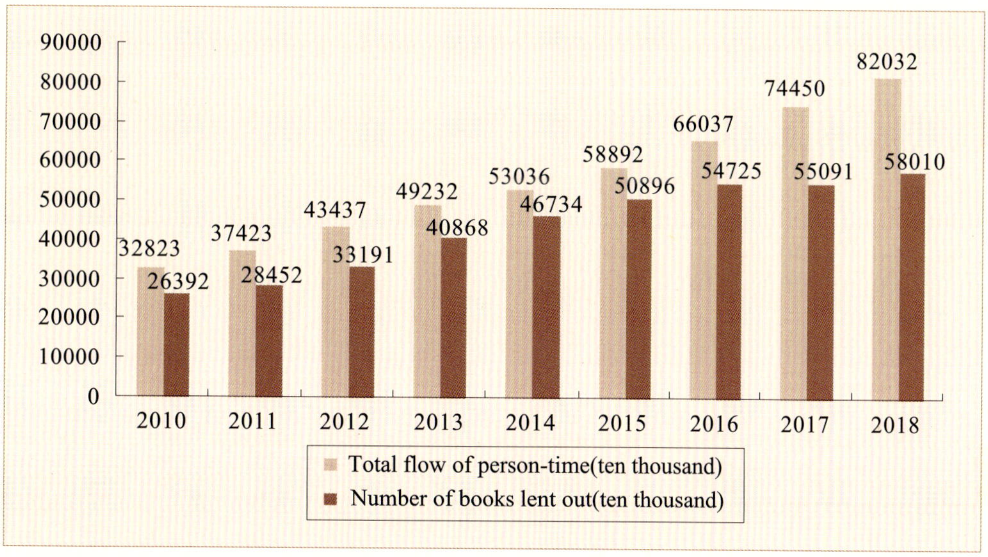

(2) Public and Community Cultural Institutions[9]

There was a total of 44,464 public and community cultural institutions across the country by the end of 2018, a decrease of 57 since the previous year. Among these, township-level comprehensive cultural stations reached a total of 33,858, a decrease of 139. By the end of the year, the total employees of public and community cultural institutions nationwide reached 185,637 an increase of 4,726 since the previous year. Staff with senior professional titles reached 6,386, accounting for 3.4%; and staffs with medium-grade professional titles reached 17,245, accounting for 9.3%.

By the end of the year, the actual floor space used by public and community institutions was 42,830,700m^2, up by 4.3% since the previous year; among them, the floor space used for offering public services was 31,461,700m^2, up by 5.7%. By the end of the year, the area covered by cultural facilities for every ten thousand people reached 306.95 m^2, an increase of 11.51 m^2 since the previous year.

Figure 4: Area of structure of national cultural facilities of mass per ten thousand people in 2010-2018

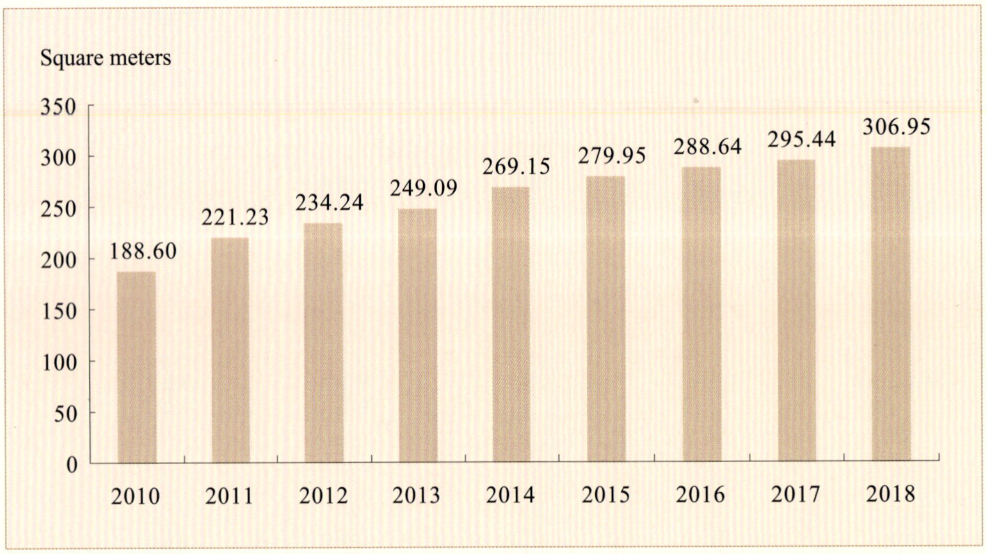

The number of activities[10] organized by nationwide public and community cultural institutions throughout the year reached 2,194,800, up by 10.9% since the previous year; total people served reached 705.53 million, up by 10.3%.

Table 2: Information of activities organized by nationwide public and community cultural institutions in 2018

	Gross		Increase over previous year (%)	
	Number of activity (ten thousand)	Number of participants (ten thousand person-time)	Number of activity	Person-time of participants
Aggregate of activities	**219.48**	**70553**	**10.9**	**10.3**
#Exhibition	15.87	11037	3.0	3.0
Cultural activities	123.12	53938	10.5	11.9
Public lecture	3.58	618	4.1	9.8
Training class	76.90	4961	13.8	10.4

By the end of the year, public and community cultural institutions nationwide fostered a total of 7,990 cultural and arts organizations[11] under cultural centers, which presented 163,000 performances to a total audience of 83.12 million. The number of amateur cultural and arts organizations supported by cultural centers (stations) totaled to 426,100, and senior citizen's community colleges set up by cultural centers reached a total of 798.

IV. Cultural and Tourism Market

In 2018, the Ministry continued to put focus on the source of issues as it encouraged culture-related businesses to improve services and image-building. We revised the administrative protocols for discredited businesses in cultural and tourism markets nationwide, conducted researches on the feasibility of the guiding opinions for travel service upgrading program and the interim regulation for online travel business operations, with the purpose of providing policy reference for improving our administrative work and building more orderly markets. 9 administrative approval items including those related to travel agencies and entertainment arcades were enlisted in the State Council's reform program of separating authorization certificates from business licenses.

We have published the Notice of the Ministry of Culture and Tourism of China on Implementing Cultural Market Management Policies in FTA Pilot Zones, and supported FTA Pilot Zones and Hainan Province to open wider their cultural and tourism markets. The national tourism supervision service platform was fully activated to further upgrade smart supervision capacity. We fostered the standard for internet cafe services and organized public contests for healthy entertainments and karaoke contests for senior citizens to upgrade the transformation of entertainment industries and internet cafes. Steady progresses have been made in ensuring security for tourists and holidays, as we invested more into security check and eliminating security hazards in travel agencies and A-level touristic sites, especially during sensitive times like the Labor Day and National Day holidays, summer holiday and flooding seasons.

By the end of the year, business units[12] in the nationwide cultural market reached 237,100, a decrease of 20,300 over the number of the previous year. They employed about 1,667,300 people, 65,900 persons less than the previous year. There were 70,584 entertainment venues across the country, with 528,200 employees in total. Throughout the year, the sales of business units in the nationwide cultural market reached 52.097 billion yuan, with a gross profit of 11.233 billion yuan. The number of internet access services reached 124,266, with 346,700 employees. Their sales totaled 29.463 billion yuan, with a gross profit of 7.676 billion yuan.

Steady progresses were seen in cultural market comprehensive policing capacity building, as we organized the second cultural market comprehensive policing professional contest, and hosted 13 workshops and online training programs for about 30,000 trainees, and more than 600 online exams as part of our efforts to step up both online and field training. The national cultural market supervision and service platform was activated and used by more than 97% of provincial, municipal and county-level policing departments. In 2018, 5.7083 million person times were checked through the platform, and 36,400 cased were closed. We have further expanded the application of mobile policing system, which was used by 143 cities across the country to run checks over 42,000 person-times and 6,880 checks of the businesses.

Further steps were made to step up market policing and regulation, as we continued to conduct targeted regulation actions to establish order in commercial performing arts, online shows, streaming music, cartoon and animation. We made more efforts to urge the closure of cases of tourism market, oversaw more than 2,000 tourist complaints, ran over 67,600 checks on travel agencies and their branches nationwide, made 3,282 cases, collected 34.81 million yuan as fines or illegal profit confiscated, and withdrew business licenses of 108 travel agencies. We actively guide and support 1+3 tourism market comprehensive overwatch system. At present, there are 437 tourism policing agencies, 344 trade bureaus specializing in tourism affairs, and 554 tourism circuit courts all over China.

V. Tourism Development

In accordance with the planning of the Central CPC Committee and the State Council of China on promoting integrated tourism, we have taken concrete steps to implement the Guiding Opinion of the General Office of the State Council on the Promotion of Integrated Tourism. In accordance with the guidelines on building role model zones of integrated tourism, we have made substantial actions to build role model zones of integrated tourism, started to formulate national measures for acceptance, authentication and management of such zones, and national standards to evaluate the acceptance of such zones. Our goal was to foster in-depth progresses of integrated tourism, and accelerate tourism transformation and upgrading.

We published the Guiding Opinions on the Promotion of Sustainable Rural Tourism and the Action Plan for Upgrading and Improving Rural Tourism Quality (2018-2020) to ensure the healthy and stable growth of rural tourism. The capacity building programs for poverty-stricken areas were augmented, as we hosted 9 tourism workshops related to poverty alleviation which trained 2,000 person-times. We also endeavored to foster stronger knowledge and skill sets of officials or backbone professionals in villages specialized in rural tourism.

Strong efforts were made to promote leisure and holiday tourism and satisfy the increasing demand of the people for traveling in leisure time, including building favorable spaces for such tourism through authenticating national-level holiday tourism destinations. We continued to endorse health tourism featuring traditional Chinese medicine, and published the list of 72 national role model zones for such tourism together with National Administration of Traditional Chinese Medicine of China. Strong efforts were made to promote self drive and RV camping tourism and accelerate standards for businesses related to such tourism. Paces were also quickened to develop hot spring and snow tourism.

Strong efforts were made to promote tourism related to revolutionary heritage of China, including launching the capacity building action to train and select best tour guides for such tourism, starting from several provinces first. In association with the Publicity Department of the CPC Central Committee, we organized contest of best tour guides of revolutionary tourism, held the showcases of “best tour guides, best stories”, and broadcasted short videos about classical revolutionary stories. We hosted 6 training workshops to train more than 1,300 officials, managers of touristic sites and travel agencies, and qualified tour guides.

We gave holistic instructions on the domestic tourism market development and promotion, launched the season for national winter tourism promotion in November, 2018, and published the notice on securing supply of winter tourism products and services. We organized the forum on winter tourism promotion work and the launching ceremony for winter tourism promotion season and snow tourism promotion. We also invited media and press to cover such events as Yangtze River international tourism belt promotion, launching ceremony of newly authenticated national-level 5A touristic sites and China Tourism Industries Exposition for wider influence.

In 2018, the domestic tourism market has seen steady growth. A slow and steady growth was observed in inbound tourism market, and fast development in outbound market. Throughout the year, 5.539 billion people made domestic visits, increasing by 10.8% over that of the previous year, and 141.20 million international visitors came to China, increasing by 1.3%. The number of outbound visitors reached 149.72 million, increased by 14.7%. The annual turnover of tourism was 5.97 trillion yuan, increased by 10.5%.

By the end of this year, there were 11,924 A-level touristic sites in China, hosting in total 6.024 billion tourists throughout the year, which was a 10.5% increase over that of the previous year. Their total turnover was 470.754 billion yuan, increased by 7.8%.

Table 3: Main Indexes of Tourism Industry (2010-2018)

Year	Domestic visitors (one hundred million)	Domestic tourism revenue (one hundred million yuan)	International visitors (ten thousand)	International tourism revenue (one hundred million dollars)	Outbound visitors (ten thousand)	Total tourism income (trillion yuan)
2010	21. 03	12580	13376	458. 14	5739	1. 57
2011	26. 41	19305	13542	484. 64	7025	2. 25
2012	29. 57	22706	13241	500. 28	8318	2. 59
2013	32. 62	26276	12908	516. 64	9819	2. 95
2014	36. 11	30312	12850	1053. 80	10728	3. 73
2015	39. 90	34195	13382	1136. 50	11689	4. 13
2016	44. 35	39390	13844	1200. 00	12203	4. 69
2017	50. 01	45661	13948	1234. 17	13051	5. 40
2018	55. 39	51278	14120	1271. 03	14972	5. 97

VI. Cultural and Tourism Industries and Related Technology

In 2018, we published the guiding opinions on promoting governmental and social capital cooperation models in cultural areas to further transform the role of government, innovate on supply mechanism in cultural areas, and encourage social capital to invest in culture. We drafted documents on promoting consumption system and mechanism, implement the awarding plan for pilot cities of cultural spending promoting, and carried out work to encourage spending on culture and tourism in an integrated way.

We have organized the 3rd cultural and arts government award for the cartoon and animation category, and gave out 20 awards to set role models for cartoon and animation creators and encourage originality. We managed to formulate two standards in digital art area, namely, the application scene, framework and metadata for digital art image monitor system and the AR demand and application framework of heritage pieces and art works, which were accepted for ITU approval. It blazed out new paths for China's digital art industry to go global. By the end of the year, there were 809 cartoon and animation enterprises jointly approved by the Ministry of Culture and Tourism, the Ministry of Finance and the State Administration of Taxation of China, among which 43 were identified as key enterprises.

We encourage private investment in culture and tourism, and published jointly with the Ministry of Finance the policy papers to promote public and private capital partnership in cultural and tourism areas. 66 culture and tourism related PPP programs jointly authenticated by the Ministry of Culture and Tourism and the Ministry of Finance were awarded financial support as incentives instead of subsidies, which totaled 364 million yuan.

We implemented the program to support entrepreneurship and business startup in cultural industries, and selected 40 qualified incubators and service platforms as receiptors of our support, aiming to build an adequate service system for entrepreneurship in private cultural businesses and small and medium-size companies. We published the interim standards for acceptance of National Role Model Parks for Cultural Industry, clearly identifying the indexes and details of acceptance work to make it more regulated. We implemented the plan to upgrade the service capacity of National Role Model Parks for Cultural Industry to support capacity building for 15 such parks.

We carried our in-depth international cooperation in cultural and creative industries for opening-up in a more adequate way. The bidding of Belt and Road priority projects for cultural trade and investment was launched, and we have confirmed to support 40 such projects as the first batch, which would leverage about 4.2 billion yuan. The program was carried out in around 10 Belt and Road countries. We hosted the cultural industry forums and policy dialogues with Canada, Viet Nam and Japan and ROK. We supported our cultural businesses to go global as groups, and organized more than 200 companies to form Chinese booths to attend 9 major international cultural fairs including the Licensing Expo in the USA. We have also coordinated the marketing and travel insurance work of the cultural and tourism sections of the 1st China International Import and Export Expo, supported the Synergy and Intersections: Forum on Culture+Technology as a new platform for business exchange and cooperation between China and the world. To strengthen training and human resource cooperation in cultural industry, we hosted the serial forum under the umbrella of Conference on Chinese Cultural Product Marketing, which trained about 2,000 cultural managers with international vision.

According to the National Bureau of Statistics, in 2018, the total turnover of 60,000 major cultural and culture related businesses reached 8925.7 billion yuan, increasing by 8.2% over that of the previous year, maintaining a fast speed of increase.

In 2018, we carried out the cultural innovation projects, and continue to evaluate the financing projects for major laboratories under the administration of our Ministry. We launched the evaluation work for 2018 national arts-related science projects, and set the important theories and realistic issues as the main direction of research. We made strong efforts to build culture and tourism think tanks, and endeavored to translate theories into practice through channels represented by Cultural and Tourism Think Tank Report, so that the research outcomes could turn into valuable reference of policies. We hosted the 3rd Lihua Cup traditional *xiqu* opera show as a collective presentation of the achievement we made in recent years in teaching young people the skill, content and culture of Chinese traditional operas.

VII. Cultural Heritage Conservation and Management

In 2018, the National Cultural Heritage Agency put the important instructions of President Xi Jinping on heritage management into practice, and implemented the opinions on further strengthening heritage management and promoting reform of heritage preservation and management to ensure that important tasks on heritage protection were completed. The overall plans to preserve the Great Wall, manage the cultural routes of the Long March and the Great Canal cultural belt development were drafted. We launched the application and evaluation work for the 8th group of national-level heritage preservation units, and started to clarify the specific bodies of such units as well as sorted out the list of provincial level units for heritage preservation. We carried out the evaluation of heritage preservation work in county-level cultural and heritage cities, further carried out prevention preservation of cultural relics in museums and preservation with the help of digital technology. Important progresses were made in underwater archaeology work in Jingyuan cruiser and Shanghai Changjiangkou II wreck, and major discoveries were made in the paleolithic remains in Tibet, Shimao in Shaanxi, Lushanmao remains and Shichengzi remains in Xinjiang.

The Internet Plus Chinese Civilization Action Plan was implemented, and the in-depth expansion of strategic cooperation with Tecent, Baidu, Netease and China Mobile was promoted. We carried out inspection on the fire control measures of museums and heritage buildings nationwide, covering 31,000 buildings and museums, and rectified more than 61, 000 defects. The action program to eliminate foul play by heritage legal persons were implemented to prosecute 673 heritage-related legal persons which violated the law, gave administrative penalties in 349 cases, urged rectification in 408 cases, penalized 314 persons for administrative ignorances and 74 persons for criminal offence. We also supervised the prosecution of several cases involving revolutionary heritage and world cultural heritage. According to the statistics by the end of 2018, there were 108 million items/sets of movable cultural heritage properties and 767,000 heritage sites in China.

By the end of the year, there were 10,160 cultural heritage institutions all over China, an increase of 229 from the previous year. Among these, 3,550 were for the preservation of cultural relics, accounting for 34.9%; and 4,918 were museums[13], accounting for 48.4%. By the end of the year, the number of employees by cultural heritage institutions reached 162,600, an increase of 1,100 compared to the end of the previous year. Among them, 9,682 were with senior professional titles, accounting for 6.0%; and 20,679 were with medium-grade professional titles, accounting for 12.7%.

Figure 5: Information of national cultural relics agencies and employed persons in 2010-2018

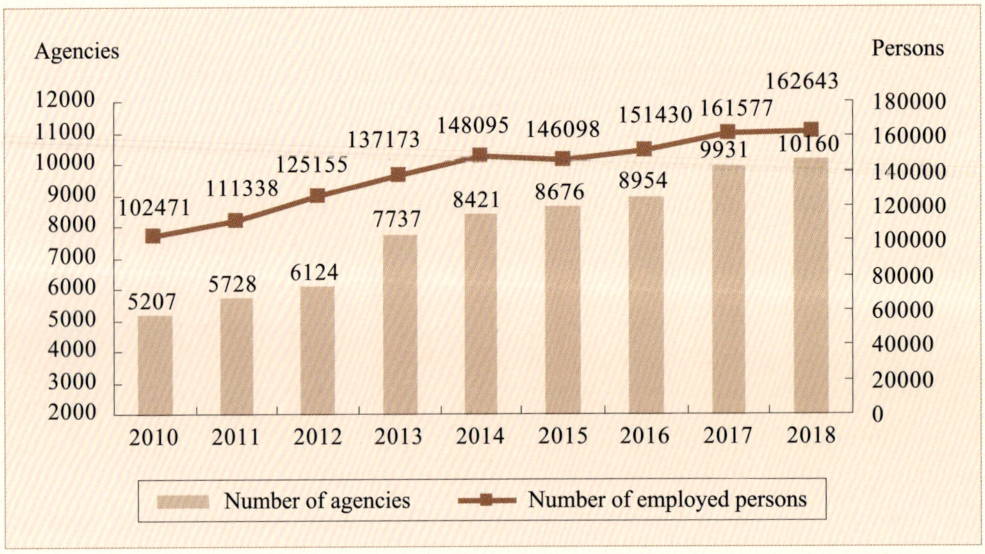

By the end of the year, there were 49.6061 million items of collections of cultural relics in the cultural heritage institutions, an increase of 1.0995 million since the end of the previous year, or up by 2.3%. Among these, the amount of collections in museums totaled to 37.5425 million, which accounted for 75.7% of the total; and for relics stores, a total of 7.514 million, accounting for 15.2%.

In 2018, 27,919 exhibitions were displayed across the country, 1,874 more than those of the previous year. Throughout the year, nationwide basic exhibitions[14] arranged by cultural heritage institutions reached 13,676, 651 more than that of the previous year; and temporary exhibitions [15] totaled 14,243, increased by 1,223; the number of visitor attendances increased to 1.22387 billion, which was an increase of 6.6% over that of the previous year. Among these, 1.4436 billion visits were to museums, accounting for 85.3% of the total visits to cultural heritage institutions, up by 7.5%. Among the visitors, the number of minors was 296.65 million, up by 2.6%, accounting for 24.2% of all visitors.

Figure 6: Person-time of audiences and minors cultural relic agencies accepting in 2010-2018

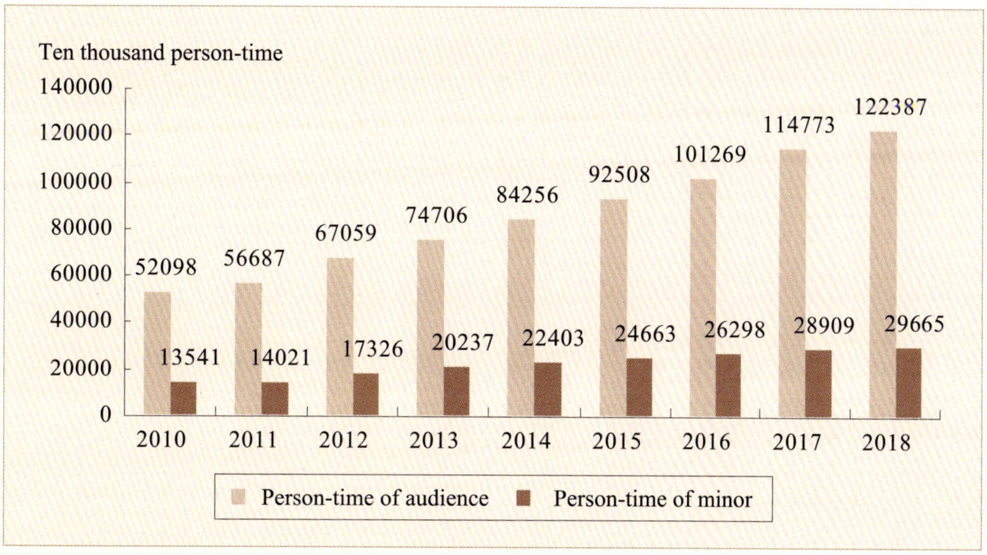

In 2018, more insurance and support were given to intangible cultural heritage (ICH) representative elements and ICH bearers, as the Sowa-Rigpa (Knowledge of Healing or Science of Healing) was inscribed in 2018 on the Representative List of the Intangible Cultural Heritage of Humanity, there were 40 Chinese items on this List. Research on national-level representative ICH elements related to cradles of Chinese civilization and culture was conducted. We archived the information of 103 national-level ICH bearers, and evaluated and accepted 253 entries in our archive which received support in 2016.

The plan to revitalize traditional craftsmanship was further implemented to enable traditional craftsmanship to better adapted to modern context. The first national-level traditional craftsmanship revitalization inventory was drafted to include 383 items in categories. We also guided the work of local governments in making the regionally inspired inventory for traditional craftsmanship, and 24 provinces, cities and prefectures has published their plans or papers in this area. We supported the traditional craftsmanship workshops to present 12 dialogues of ICH bearers, and facilitated the crossover cooperation between ICH bearers and businesses and colleges.

The research and training work mechanism was further improved to cover more areas and the ICH bearer workshop and training program was carried out in an in-depth way, as we published the action plan (2018-2020) for this program, identifying 112 colleges and universities as partners of 2018. Across China, 628 training sessions were conducted to train 26,500 person times. In total 95,000 person times were trained in collateral programs at local level. We continued to explore pilot programs for training bearers of newly authenticated ICH elements, and supported Minzu University of China to organize training programs and forums of ICH bears of folklore and literature in Hubei province.

We authenticated and published the name list of 1,082 national-level representative ICH bearers, which was the 5th group of such bearers. By the end of 2018, there were 3,068 national-level representative ICH bearers and 1,372 national-level representative ICH elements. Further efforts were made in enhancing preservation and management facilities of national-level representative ICH elements, as 201 million yuan from the central budget was allocated to support the infrastructure to safeguard and manage 26 national-level representative ICH elements with the aim to better integrate ICH safeguarding with the economic and social development.

The broadcasting channels and models were innovated to upgrade ICH publicity quality and raise social awareness across China to transmit the best of our traditional culture. We organized the 2018 Cultural and Natural Heritage Day, rolling out more than 3,700 large and medium-scale ICH showcases nationwide. We held the national quyi (traditional opera, folklore and storytelling) week as a collective showcase of 127 national-level representative ICH elements in quyi category. We produced and streamed the videos of ICH lectures to publicize ICH safeguarding tenets and ICH knowledge. Promotional events such as ICH image exhibition, fashion show and lecture tours were organized to attract 260 million audience attendances online and on site. Focusing on making heritage alive in modern context, the 5th China ICH Expo was organized to celebrate the success of China in safeguarding ICH in recent years. The Expo attracted 820,000 visitor attendances and about 60 million views online. We supported and guided local governments and institutions to publicize ICH on campus, in classrooms and through textbooks so that the young generation can be ICH aware.

By the end of 2018, there were a total of 2,467 safeguarding units for intangible cultural heritage across the country, with 17,308 employees. Throughout the year in the country, these units held 65,495 showcases with 49.60 million visitor attendances, up by 20.6% and by 16.6%

respectively. They hosted 16,844 folklore activities (up by 24.0%) with 48.50 million visitor attendances (up by 0.7%).

VIII. International Cultural and Tourism Exchange and Bonding with Hong Kong, Macao and Taiwan Regions

In 2018, giving full play to our bilateral cultural and tourism mechanism as well as high-level people-to-people dialogues with other countries, we have signed cultural agreements or executive programs with 18 countries including Gambia, Panama, Spain and Nigeria for stronger exchange and cooperation with our global partners. We hosted events related to SHO, Japan and ROK, US and ASEAN, and participated in conferences with Italy, Russia, Mongolia, and Eurasian, Asia-Pacific and BRICS meetings.

"Belt and Road" cultural and tourism exchange mechanism was built, and Silk Road leagues of international theaters, museums, art festivals, libraries and art museums were established. The Ministry also hosted the 5th Silk Road International Art Festival, the 2nd Silk Road (Dunhuang) International Cultural Expo and Exhibition of Art Museum Collections of Silk Road Countries. Brand exchange programs including Silk Road Cultural Tour and Silk Road Cultural Messenger to cement the foundation for connectivity along the Belt and Road.

In 2018, Happy Chinese New Year Celebrations presented more than 2,000 festivities at 400 plus cities in over130 countries across the globe, making it one of the most visible external cultural brands of China that tells the stories of China through culture. The Ministry also invested more to promote China as a destination through programs named China Beyond Imagination and Beautiful China. Focus on China activities were hosted under the umbrellas of Le Festival d'Avignon and Edinburgh Fringe, and Chinese cultural years (festivals) were also organized in such countries as the US, Canada, Russia and Nepal for strong Chinese festive presence across the globe.

The guidelines for the Ministry of Culture and Tourism and local governments of China to co-establish China Cultural Centers overseas was formulated as part of our efforts to strengthen the regulation structure of overseas cultural and tourism agencies delegated by Chinese government. In 2018, with 2 newly launched China Cultural Centers in Latvia and Morocco respectively, the total number of China Cultural Centers overseas reached 37. Inter-governmental agreements were signed between China and 6 countries including Jordan, Uruguay, UAE, Côte d'Ivoire, Algeria and Spain. To continue cooperation with local governments, the Ministry also signed agreements with Guangxi Zhuang Autonomous Region and Jiangxi Province to jointly build China Cultural Centers in Hanoi and Lisbon respectively. We also guided overseas China Cultural Centers across the world to present China Cultural Week and Mid-autumn Day celebrations in a concerted way.

Cultural and tourism bonding with Hong Kong, Macao and Taiwan was carried out in an active way, including advancements in building coordination mechanism for cultural and tourism development in the Guangdong-Hong Kong-Macao Greater Bay Area (GBA). The Ministry hosted the 9th Cross-Strait Cultural & Creative Industry Expo, the14th Strait Travel Fair and the 11th Cross-Strait Cultural Industries Fair; expanded the visibility of theme cultural events such as Xiangjiang Mingyueye Mid-autumn Day Gala and Cross-Strait Folklore Temple Fair; continue to carry out cultural exchange programs such as Yihailiujin (literally, interflow across the golden sea of arts) and Qingxi Qiantang cross-strait cultural tour; organized tourism promotions including field trips of Hong Kong and Macau travel agencies to Gansu Province; and hosted cross-strait travel fair in summer in Taipei. We also continued to encourage young people from Hong Kong, Macau and Taiwan to identify with Chinese culture through their cultural tours and study tours in Chinese mainland.

The year saw 3,383 international cultural exchange programs approved by government cultural departments with 66,734 participant attendances; 490 cultural bonding programs with Hong Kong and Macau, with 11,411 participant attendances, and 311 cultural bonding programs with Taiwan with 3,642 participant attendances.

IX. Investment

In 2018, the central budget of China continued to subsidize local culture by implementing cultural projects, such as free access to museums, libraries, and cultural centers (stations), intangible cultural heritage safeguarding, digital cultural contents for public use and cultural infrastructure development at city-level. It provided special funding in total 5.051 billion yuan, down by 0.6% compared to that of the previous year.

Figure 7: Information of subvention of central authority to local cultural projects in 2010-2018

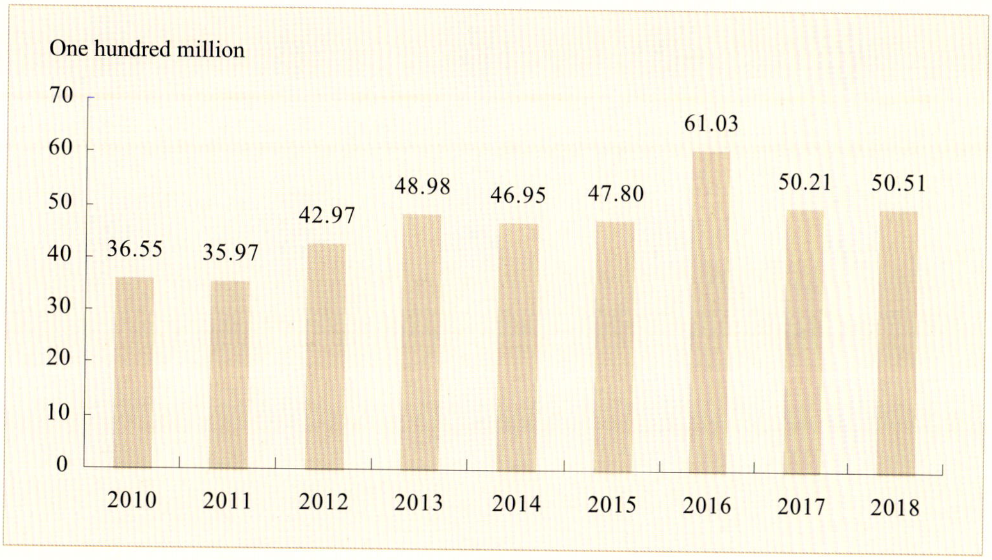

The central budget also allocated 1.485 billion yuan for tourism development, mainly supporting toilet upgrading in local-level touristic sites, role model zones for integrated tourism and the transformation and upgrading of tourism industry as well as public service system for tourism.

The total amount of cultural undertaking expenses[16] for the whole year was 92.833 billion yuan, an increase of 7.253 billion yuan over that of the previous year, up by 8.5%; as for the national cultural undertaking expenses per capita, the total was 66.53 yuan, an increase of 4.96 yuan over the previous year, up by 8.1%.

Figure 8: Information of cultural operating expenses per capita in 2010-2018

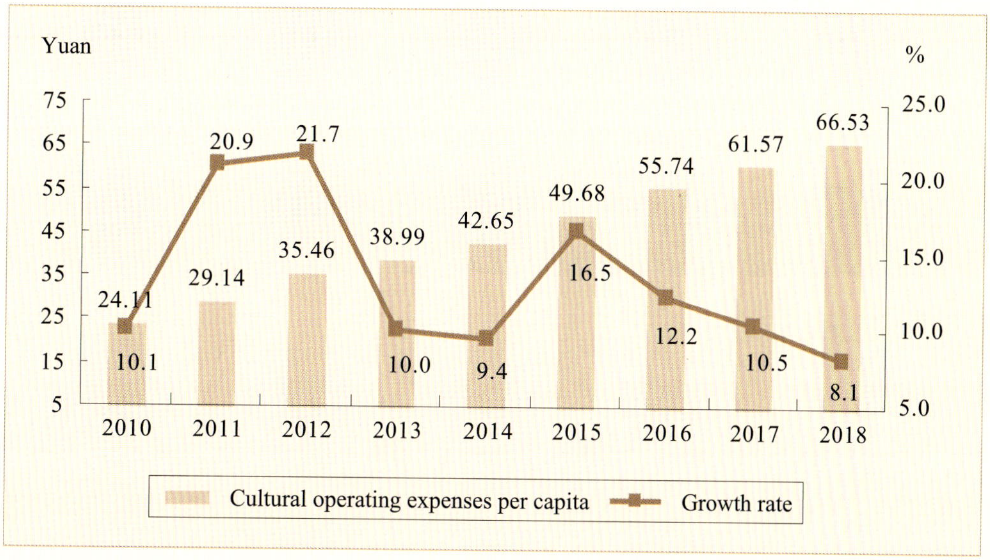

The national cultural undertaking expenses accounted for 0.42% of the country's total financial expenditure, same with that of the previous year.

Figure 9: Proportion of national cultural operating expense in financial expenditure

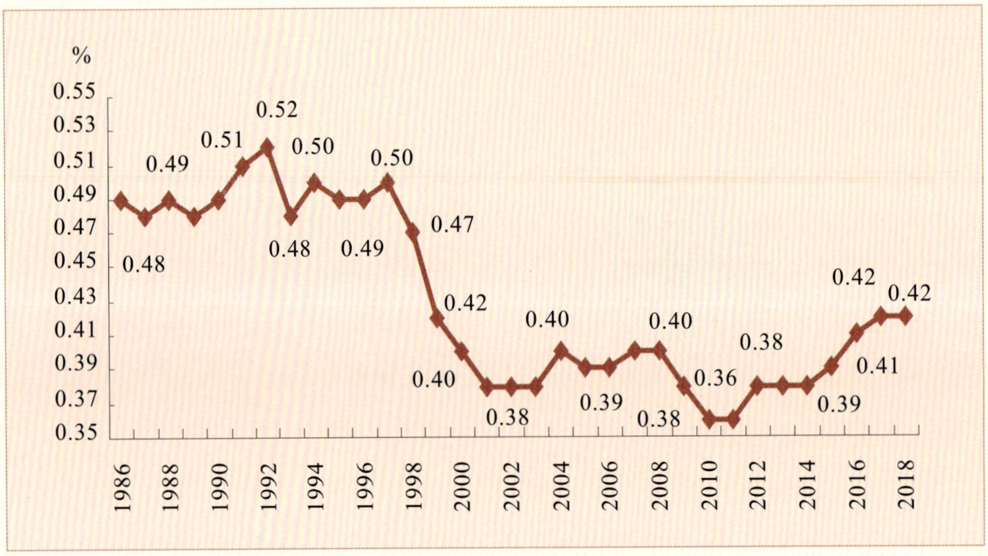

Regarding the national cultural undertaking expenses, that of cultural units above county level was 42.496 billion yuan, accounting for 45.8%, 0.7 percentage points lower than that of the previous year; that of cultural units of county level or below the level of county was 50.337 billion yuan, accounting for 54.2%, up by 0.7 percentage points in the sense of its proportion. The cultural undertaking expenses of eastern region[17] reached 41.624 billion yuan, accounting for 44.8%, and its proportion increased by 0.2%; that of central region reached 23.271 billion yuan, accounting for 25.1%, its proportion increased by 0.2%; and that of western region reached 24.293 billion yuan, accounting for 26.2%, its proportion decreased by 0.8%.

The amount of maintenance expenses of national cultural heritage[18] was 37.879 billion yuan, an increase of 2.957 billion yuan, up by 8.3% over that of the previous year; the maintenance expenses of national cultural heritage accounted for 0.17% of China's total financial expenditures, same with that of the previous year.

Table 4: Urban & Rural and Regional-based distribution of national cultural undertaking expenses

		In 1995	In 2000	In 2005	In 2010	In 2015	In 2017	In 2018
Aggregate (one hundred million yuan)	**Nationwide**	**33.39**	**63.16**	**133.82**	**323.06**	**682.97**	**855.80**	**928.33**
	# Above county level	24.44	46.33	98.12	206.65	352.84	398.35	424.96
	County level and below level of county	8.95	16.87	35.70	116.41	330.13	457.45	503.37
	# Eastern region	13.43	28.85	64.37	143.35	287.87	381.71	416.24
	Central region	9.54	15.05	30.58	78.65	164.27	213.30	232.71
	Western region	8.30	13.70	27.56	85.78	193.87	230.70	242.93
Proportion (%)	**Nationwide**	**100.0**	**100.0**	**100.0**	**100.0**	**100.0**	**100.0**	**100.0**
	# Above county level	73.2	73.4	73.3	64.0	51.7	46.5	45.8
	County level and below level of county	26.8	26.7	26.7	36.0	48.3	53.5	54.2
	# Eastern region	40.2	45.7	48.1	44.4	42.1	44.6	44.8
	Central region	28.6	23.8	22.9	24.3	24.1	24.9	25.1
	Western region	24.9	21.7	20.6	26.6	28.4	27.0	26.2

According the Ministry of Finance, in 2018, the central budget spent 35.22 billion yuan on culture, sports and media[19] undertakings, 3.7% more than that of the previous year, accounting for 1.59% of the total expenditure, 0.07 percentage points less than that of the previous year.

Figure 10: Aggregate and growth rate of expenditure of national culture, sports and media in 2010-2018

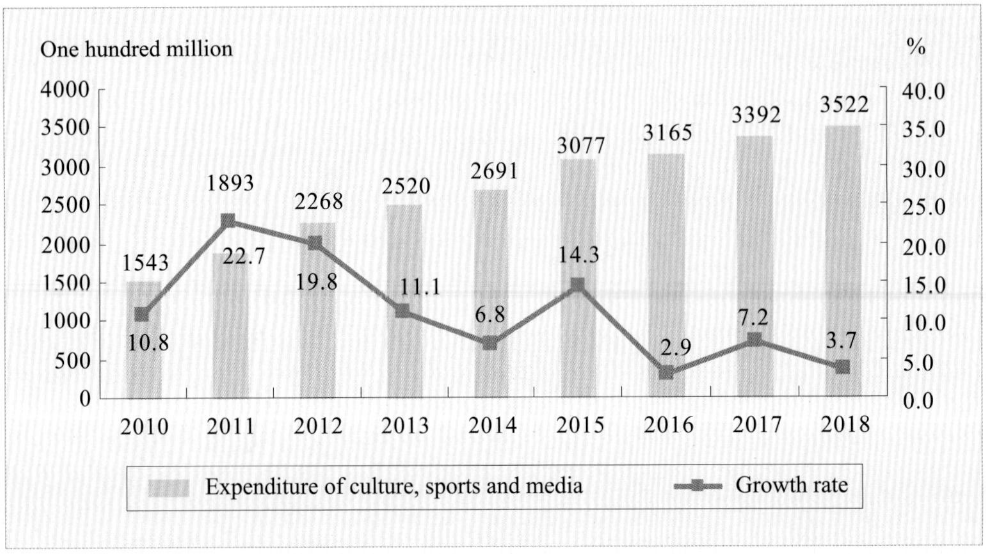

Notes:

[1] All the data of the communiqué are preliminary statistical data. HKSAR, MSAR, and Taiwan Province are not included in each data. Some of data are not compatible with the total of subentries due to rounding off.

[2] Cultural and tourism units refers to cultural institutions that national cultural and tourism departments of all levels organize or implement industrial management, excluding cultural institutions organized or managed by the departments of all levels of press and publications, radio , film and television, etc. According to the current statistical system, the cultural institutions (such as public libraries, cultural centers, cultural stations, museums, etc.) organized by cultural departments are brought into the statistical range. Regarding cultural institutions with industrial management, the private art performance troupes, cybercafé, and entertainment venues are brought into statistical range, while the mechanism of exchange of works of art, internet culture institution are not in the range.

[3] The employees refer to the people who work and receive working rewards in the institutions that cultural and tourism departments at all levels organize or implement industrial management.

[4] The art performance troupes mean various professional artistic performance organizations

which are organized by cultural and tourism institutions or to which the cultural institutions implement industrial management (with approval of cultural administration department and commercial performance license), and is engaged in such activities as performing arts.

[5] Public library refers to all kinds of institutions that are organized by cultural and tourism departments at all levels, and is open to public as well as providing popularization and education of science, culture, and other knowledge.

[6] The total collection of books in public libraries refers to the sum of audiovisual literature materials including bound volume, manual, manuscript, micro-reproduction, videotape, audio tape and CD of ancient books, books, periodicals and newspapers in catalogue. It does not include digital books.

[7] The number of library cards issued refers to the number of library cards which are issued by public libraries and used at least once in that very year.

[8] The total flow of person-time of public library refers to the gross person-time of receiving the service of the libraries in that year, including borrowing books, consultation and participating in various readers' activities.

[9] The cultural institutions for mass public and communities refer to the places that cultural and tourism departments at all levels organize for mass cultural activities, mainly including cultural centers (including comprehensive cultural center and mass art gallery) and cultural stations.

[10] The number of activities means the sum of the organizations of cultural literary and artistic activities, training classes, exhibitions, and public lectures.

[11] The literature and art groups refer to performance teams composed by the staff of this institution and that provide performances for the mass.

[12] The operating units of cultural markets refer to the agencies which are approved or filed by administrative departments of cultural markets and have relevant licenses and filing documents, and that engage in cultural management and services. In line with the current statistical systems, the statistical range of operating units of the cultural market only include private art performance troupes, entertainment venues, and business sites of internet access services.

[13] The museum refers to the non-profit and permanent social service institution which

collects, preserves, and exhibits the witness of human activity and natural environment with intent of research, education, and appreciation, as well as being open to the public. It includes the units that carry out activities with proper names such as museums, memorial halls, science and technology museums, exhibition halls, etc.

[14] The permanent exhibition refers to the exhibition which is displayed in the pavilion, with fixed location and for an extended time.

[15] The temporary exhibition means the multi-formed exhibition which is set in the institution and designed by the pavilion.

[16] Cultural undertaking expense means aggregate of expenditures that the finance of all levels in the area invests to the organizer of cultural and tourism systems. According to current statistical caliber, cultural operating expense does not include administrative operation expenditures of cultural and tourism administration and management departments at all levels.

[17] Eastern region includes Beijing, Tianjin, Liaoning Province, Shanghai, Jiangsu Province, Fujian Province, Shandong Province, and Guangdong Province; Central region includes Hebei Province, Shanxi Province, Jilin Province, Heilongjiang Province, Anhui Province, Jiangxi Province, Henan Province, Hubei Province, Hunan Province and Hainan Province; Western region includes Inner Mongolia (autonomous region), Guangxi Province, Chongqing, Sichuan Province, Guizhou Province, Yunan Province, Tibet (autonomous region), Shannxi Province, Gansu Province, Qinghai Province, Ningxia (autonomous region), and Xinjiang (autonomous region).

[18] The maintenance expenses of national cultural heritage refer to the aggregate of expenditures that the finance departments at all levels in the area invest to the operation of cultural relics. It generally includes financial appropriation (excluding appropriation of capital construction) of operation institutions of cultural relic such as museum, protection and management agencies for cultural relics, etc. and financial subsidies of enterprises subordinate to cultural relic departments.

[19] The data of expenditure of culture, sports and media, which originates from the Ministry of Finance, is the investment of government at all levels in culture, cultural relics, sports, radio, film and television, and press and publications.